AF262868

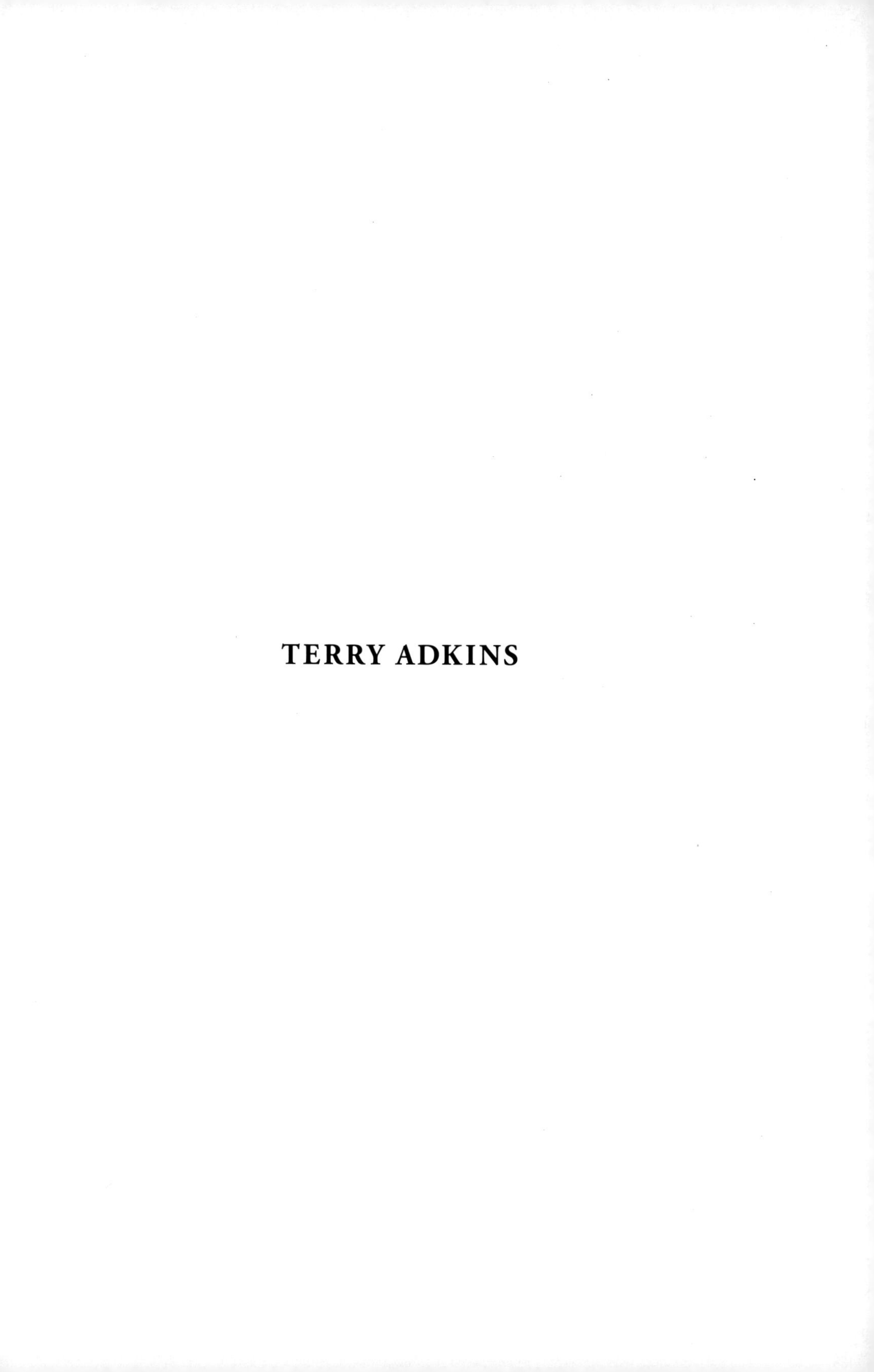

TERRY ADKINS

TERRY ADKINS

Soldier Shepherd Prophet Martyr
Videos from 1998–2013

Edited by Kendra Paitz
University Galleries of Illinois State University
2017

CONTENTS

—

CURATORIAL STATEMENT

by Kendra Paitz

Soldier Shepherd Prophet Martyr: Videos from 1998–2013, the first survey of videos by Terry Adkins (1953–2014), featured twelve videos—some created to be standalone works and others developed for inclusion in his performances and multimedia "recital" installations—as well as documentation of the artist's 2013 Lone Wolf Recital Corps performances at The Studio Museum in Harlem. The exhibition's title was derived from a phrase repeated throughout *Hiving Be (Apis mellifera)* (1998–1999), the earliest video in the exhibition. Adkins combined these four powerful words—which resonate with historical, religious, and political tones—to reference abolitionist John Brown, the focus of the video, but they can also provide a poetic lens through which to view the other videos and the late artist himself, a fearless performer and dedicated educator who often cited his intense belief that "art can be a force for change."

Adkins, who received an M.S. degree in Printmaking from Illinois State University's School of Art, ingeniously united the improvisation of a jazz musician and the deep research of a conceptual artist in his seamless blending of performance, sound, sculpture, printmaking, photography, and video. He studied historical figures that he deemed "immortal"—including John Brown, Jimi Hendrix, Martin Luther King Jr., Bessie Smith, Matthew Henson, and Ludwig van Beethoven, often focusing on moments and biographical facts that have escaped our collective memories and the dominant narratives of his subjects' lives. Saying that he was drawn to figures with "exceptional human stories" whose "legacies are still very alive," Adkins created commanding works about revolutionary spirits who triumphed over adversity and effected meaningful change. For example, his *Synapse (from Black Beethoven)*—in which a

framed portrait of Beethoven slowly transitions from a traditional Caucasian depiction toward one that shows him with darker skin and hair as a tense instrumental soundtrack drones in the background—acknowledges questions about Beethoven's Moorish ancestry while also honoring that he composed his most influential works after suffering severe hearing loss.

The exhibition presented Adkins' videos together and independently from any related two- or three-dimensional works, offering the viewer the opportunity for a close examination of the strategies the artist used, from constructing split-screen videos comprised of recorded and found footage, to animating images from archival stereo cards, to recording actions in real time. Although he made videos throughout his career, these remain lesser-known than his performances and sculptures like *Muffled Drums*, a ceiling-scraping stack of silent but previously played bass drums, or *Aviarium*, a recent series that magnifies the wavelengths of various birds' songs and manifests them in silver-plated brass cymbals and trumpet mutes. Akin to the existing objects populating his sculptural works, several of Adkins' videos feature found footage or archival imagery. Rather than narrative accounts, they are vibrant combinations of (often abstract) visual references to the chosen figures that are activated through recitation, song, and even silence. Importantly, the heavy influence of music is evident not only in the soundtracks and Adkins' selection of musicians and composers as some of his subjects, but in the structure and composition of the videos—the rhythmic interactions between images in double- and triple-channel works, the cadence of interposed blank spaces, and the recurrent vibrating stereoscopic imagery that pulsates with life.

Hiving Be (Apis mellifera)

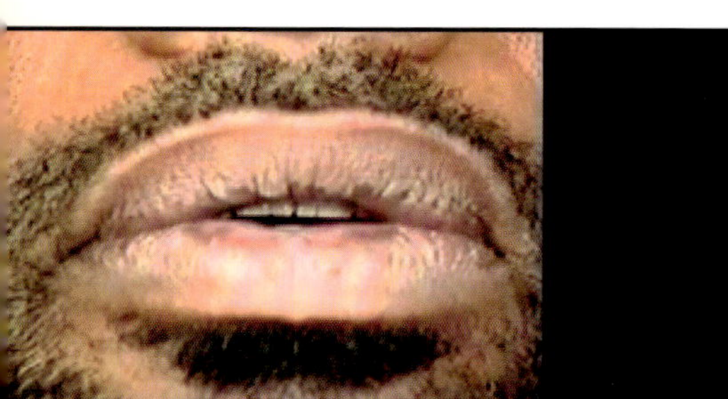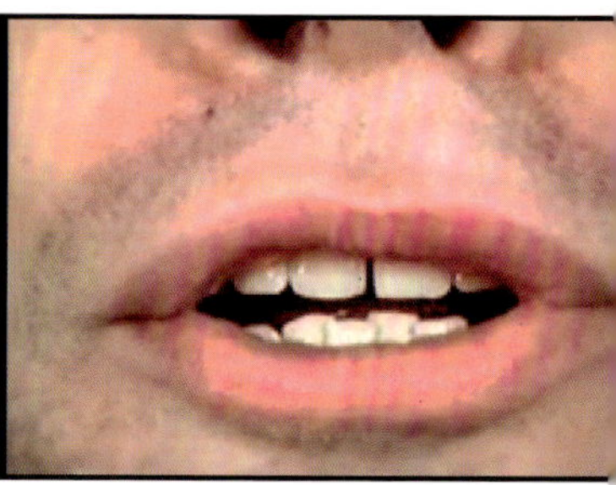

1998–1999. Digital video with sound (originally presented as a three-channel video on monitors). 9:36 minutes.

Hiving Be (Apis mellifera), the first of Adkins' three videos related to abolitionist John Brown (1800–1859), was made on the grounds of the John Brown House in Akron, Ohio. On October 16, 1859, Brown led a raid on the federal arsenal at Harpers Ferry, Virginia. The multiracial group of 22 men, which included one freed slave and one fugitive slave, hoped to gain access to weapons and supplies to arm a slave rebellion.[1] Brown was captured, tried for and convicted of treason, and later hanged for his actions. "Hiving bees" was the code name for the raid and "Apis mellifera" is the scientific name for a honey bee.[2]

In the video, the mouths of Adkins and a Caucasian man are shown in close-up as they repeatedly chant the words "soldier, shepherd, prophet, martyr" to draw attention to varying historical views of the abolitionist. Their recitation is accompanied by the sounds of buzzing bees, rolling thunder, and ringing bells. Meanwhile, images of bells, fleece, bees, and honey—references to Brown's life as a shepherd and his self-sacrificial mission to end slavery— fade into and out of the three sections on the screen. Over the course of the video, the images of the two men slowly fade from full-color to black-and-white, perhaps to further acknowledge Brown's pursuit of racial unity.

1. See http://www.civilwar.org/hallowed-ground-magazine/Fall-09/john-browns-raiders.html for information about "John Brown's Raiders."

2. Adkins, Terry. "Why the Civil War Still Matters to American Artists." Lecture at Smithsonian American Art Museum, Washington, D.C., March 2013.

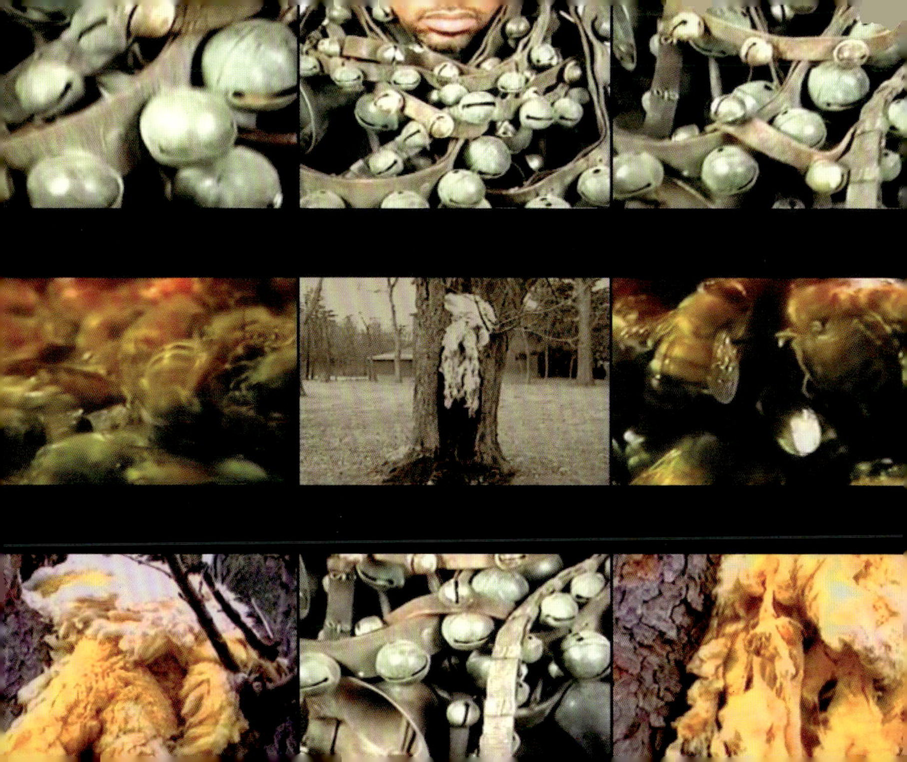

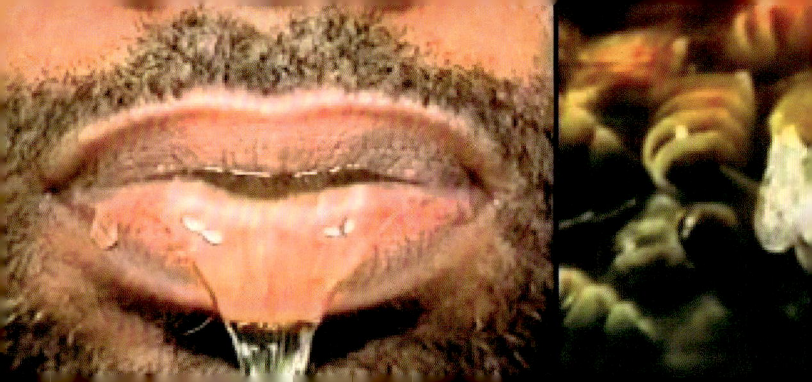

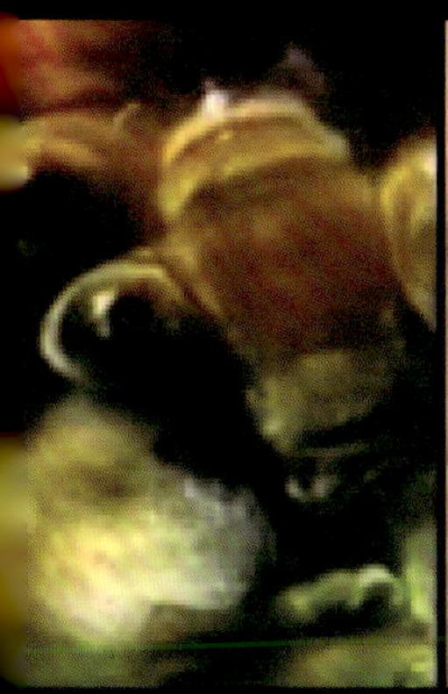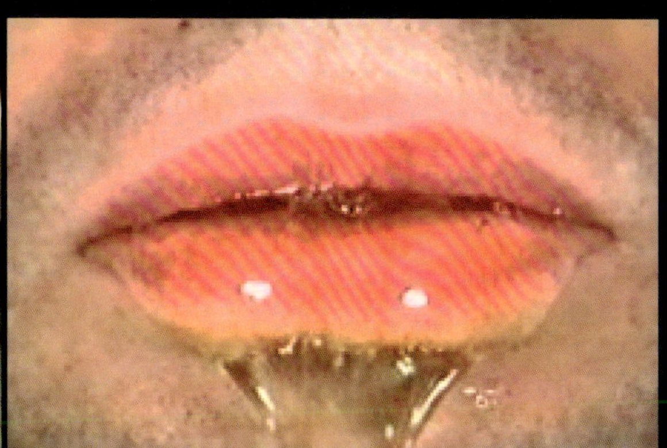

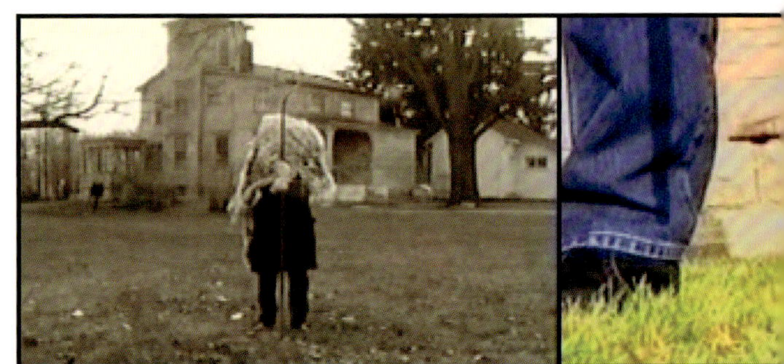

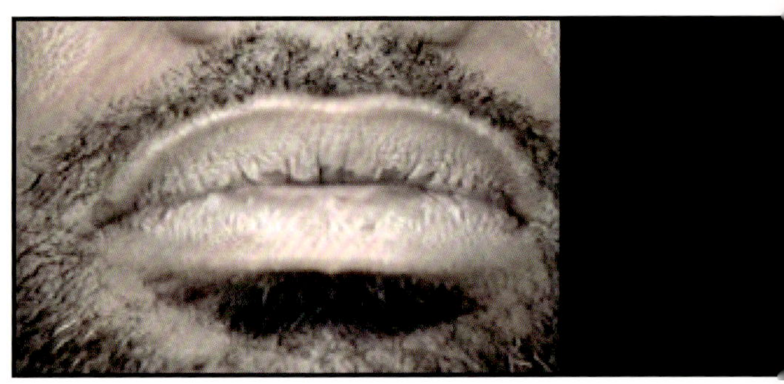

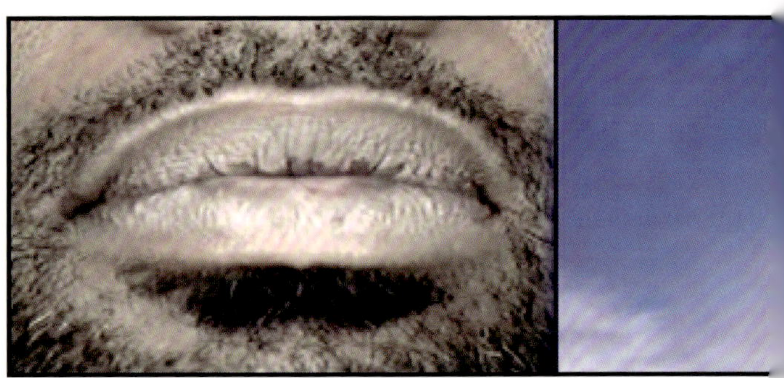

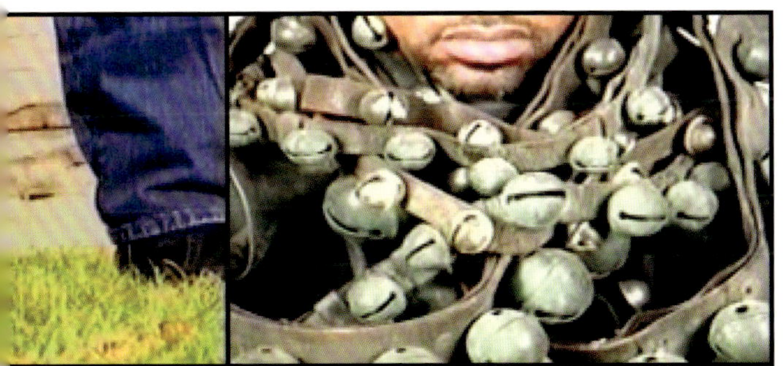

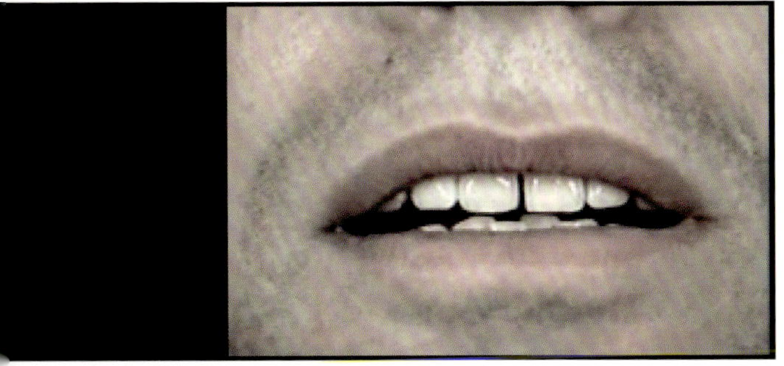

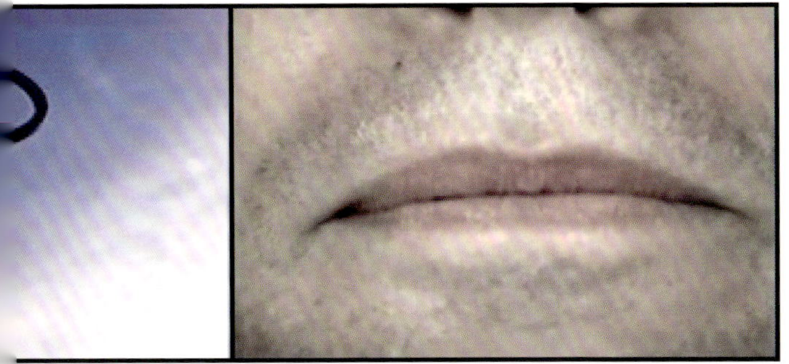

Hiving Be (Apis mellifera)

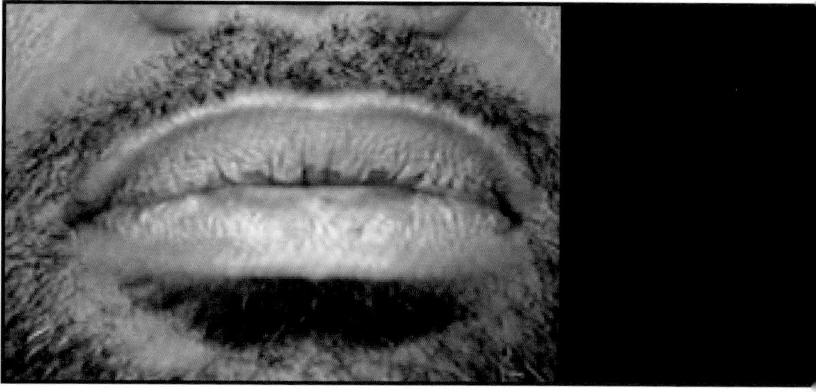

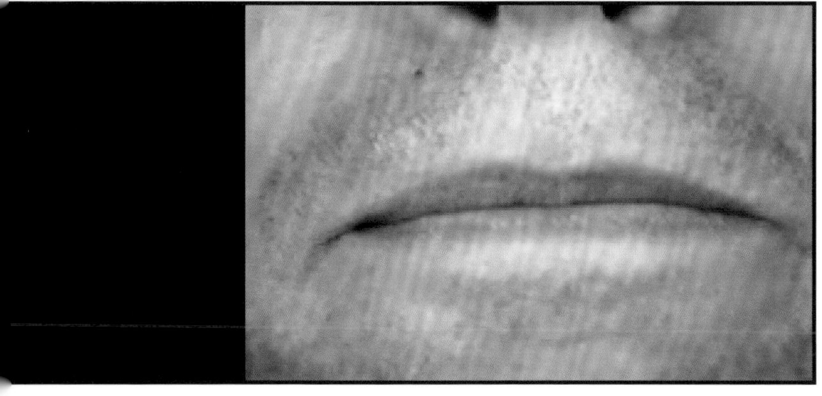

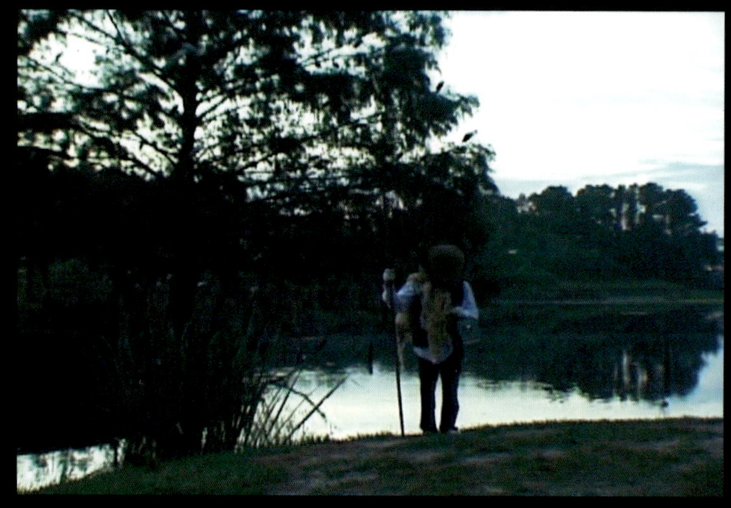

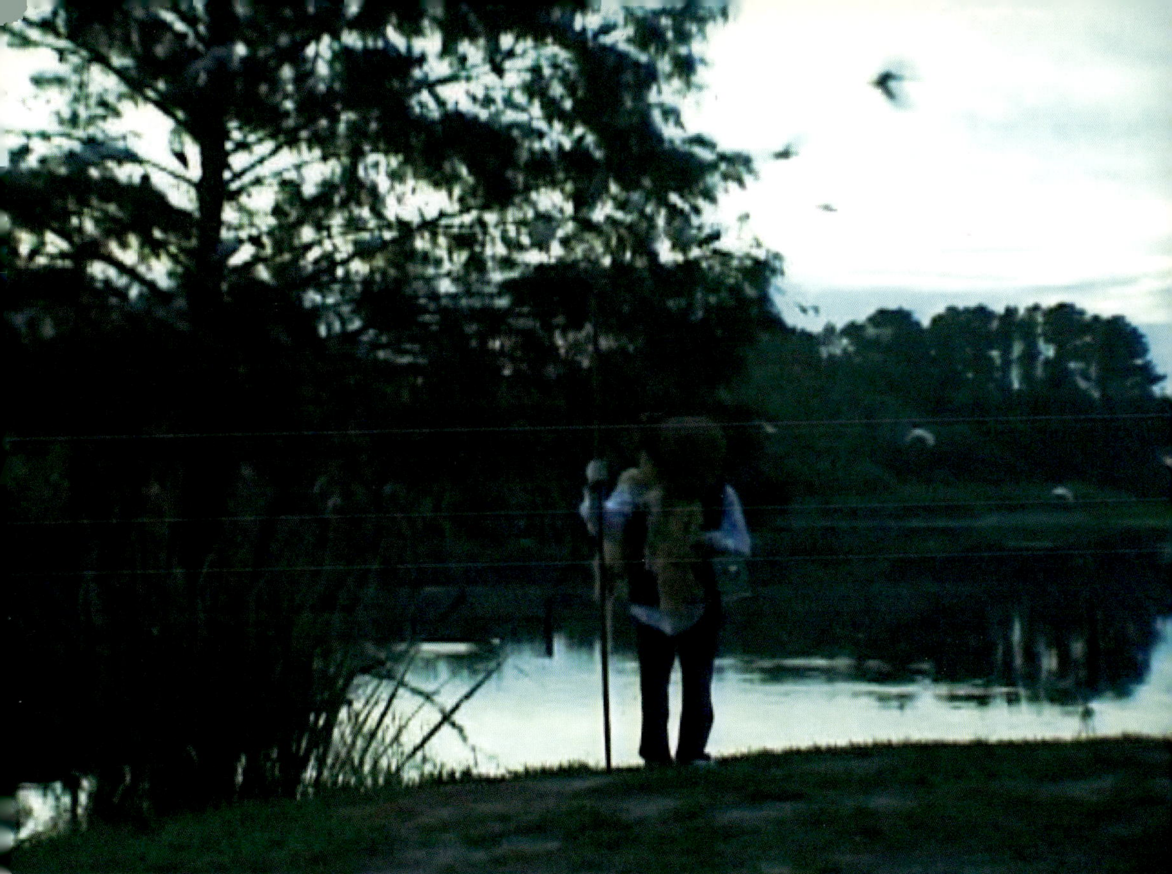

Roost

—

2001. Single-channel
digital video with sound.
9:09 minutes.

1. Drake, Cathryn. Review of *Meteor
Stream*, by Terry Adkins, American
Academy in Rome. *Artforum
International*, May 2010.

2. Gaines, Charles. "The Last Recital:
Terry Adkins." *Mousse Magazine* 43
(March 2013): 182–189.

3. Finley, Cheryl. "Imagined History:
The Work of Terry Adkins." *Nka:
Journal of Contemporary African Art*
19 (Summer 2004): 50–54.

In *Roost*, Adkins' second video devoted to John Brown, the artist imagines an alternate history in which Brown's group kept gaining members and strength as they moved southward before eventually declaring victory in the swamps of Florida. Adkins appears as the spirit of Brown on the banks of Lake Alice in Gainesville, Florida.[1] He wears a fleece beard and holds a staff to reference Brown's role as an actual shepherd with an Ohio sheep farm and as a metaphorical shepherd for the anti-slavery campaign. He also wears a basket over his head as a nod to anonymity strategies "employed by early Japanese assassins."[2] We hear the ambient sounds of birds' songs, a gentle breeze, and the occasional rumble of distant cars as a flock of white birds gracefully flies into and out of a large tree, seemingly oblivious to the mysterious figure who peacefully asserts his presence among them. In an analysis of Adkins' *Deeper Still* body of work (which includes *Roost*), art historian Cheryl Finley wrote, "Adkins' ghost of John Brown shimmers as a reminder of the past and a portent of the future."[3]

2004–2012. Single-channel
digital video with sound.
18:01 minutes.

Synapse *(from Black Beethoven)*

In *Synapse (from Black Beethoven)*, a framed portrait of Ludwig van
Beethoven (1770–1827) fills the screen as a tense instrumental
soundtrack drones in the background. Slowly and seamlessly, the
composer's skin tone, hair, and features shift from the traditional
Caucasian depiction of the legendary figure toward one that shows
him with darker skin and hair. The portrait shifts ever so slightly
back to its original state before it begins another mysterious
round of transformation. Beethoven seems to be trapped in an
endless cycle of becoming, with the construction of his biography
still up for debate.

Although Adkins was interested in questions of Beethoven's
Moorish ancestry, he was more invested in celebrating the fact that
the composer overcame deafness—the removal of the sense
most connected to his musical gift—and reached generations of
people with his symphonies.[1] Adkins said he was exploring
the "idea of remembering what it's like to hear" so "the morphing
of the images is very subtle, but the sound is very physical."[2] The
artist created the music using an old upright bass and a computer-
based electronic processor.[3]

1. Adkins, Terry and George Lewis.
"Event Scores: Terry Adkins and George
Lewis in Conversation." *Artforum
International*, March 2014, 244–253.

2. Ibid.

3. Author's conversation with Joshua
Mosley on November 23, 2015.

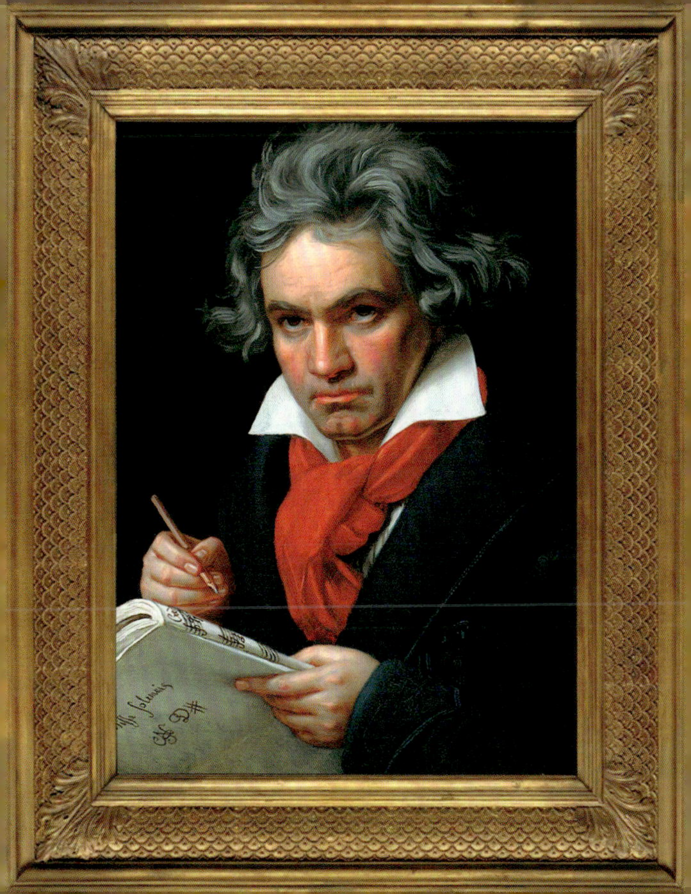
Missa solemnis
D#

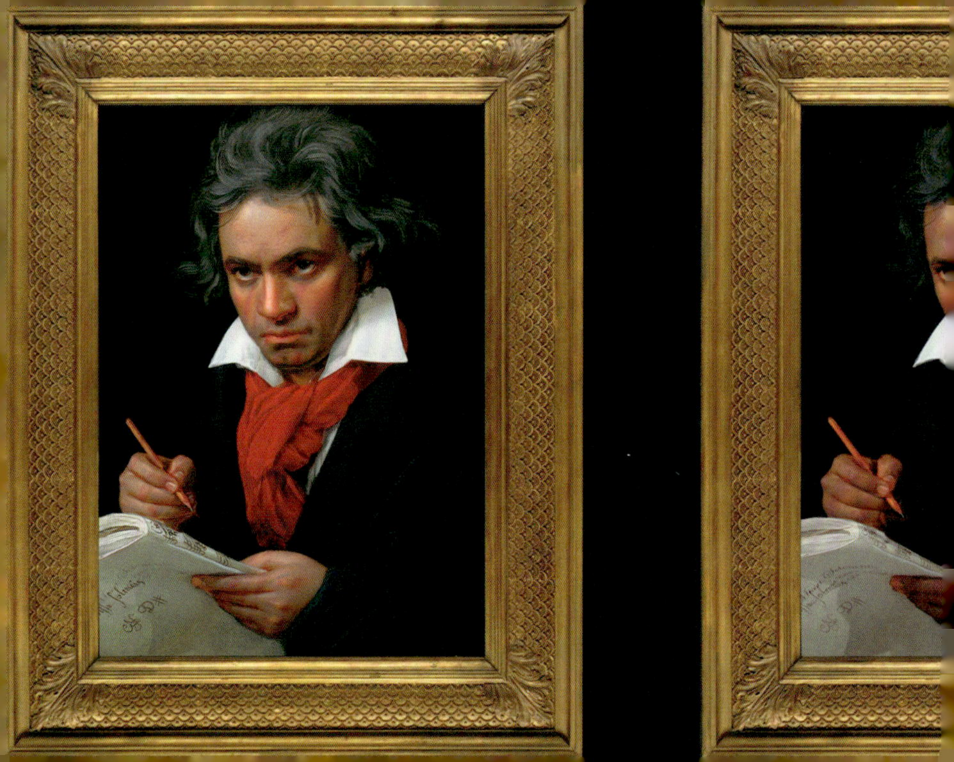

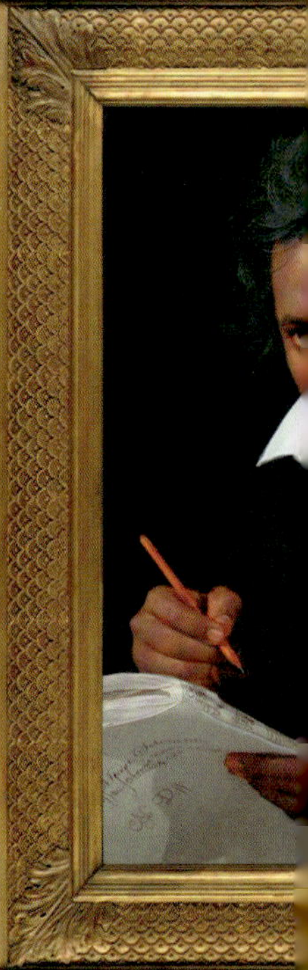

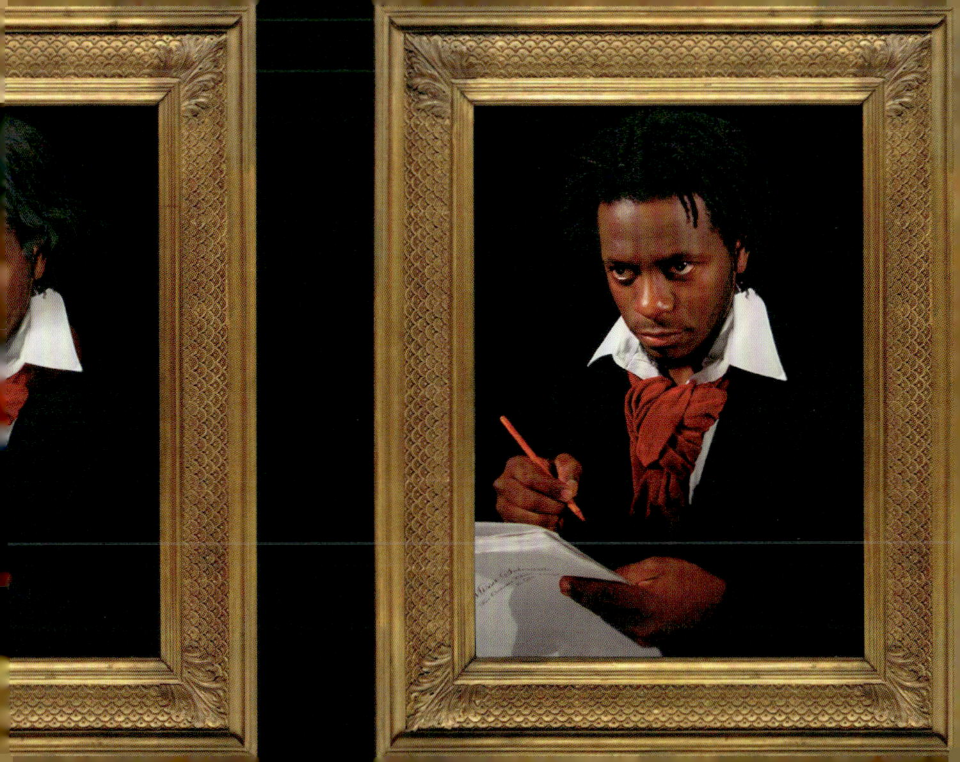

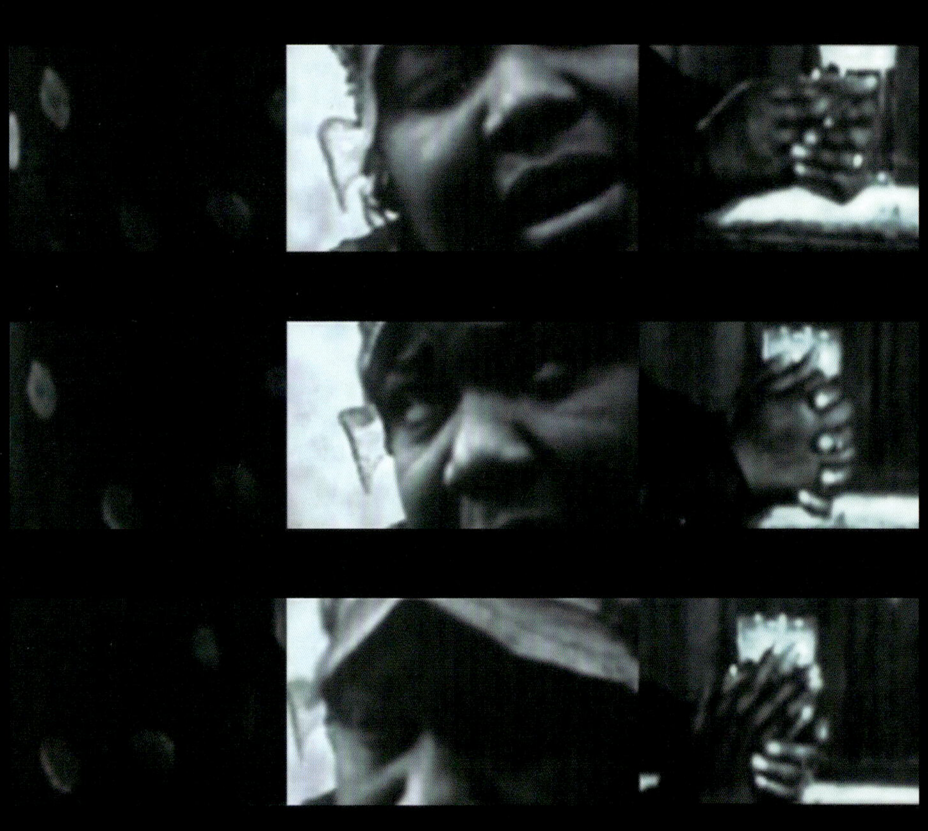

Mute

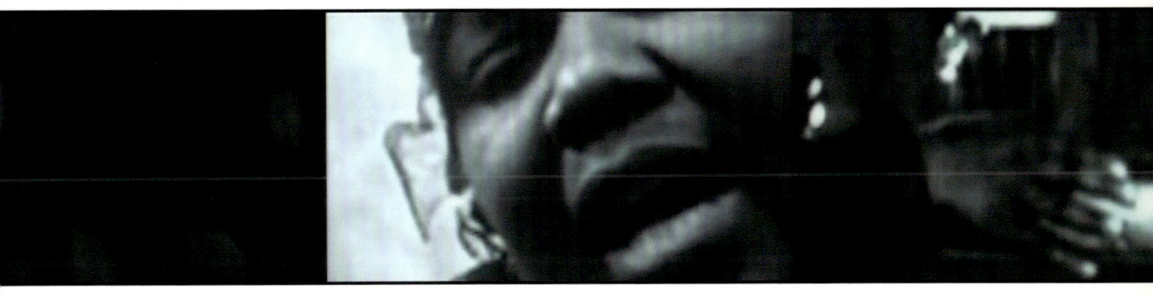

2007–2011. Single-channel
digital video, silent.
22:07 minutes.

1. Mark Cantor, "St. Louis Blues,"
Library of Congress, accessed on
June 13, 2016. https://www.loc.
gov/programs/static/national-film-
preservation-board/documents/
st_louis_blues.pdf.

This silent black-and-white video shows three views of American
singer Bessie Smith (1894–1937) captured from *St. Louis Blues*,
a 1929 film produced by W.C. Handy. A portion of Smith's polka-
dotted dress and a pair of (repeatedly folding) hands frame
a tightly cropped image of the groundbreaking "Empress of the
Blues" rolling her head as she sings a heartfelt song we cannot
hear. Smith recorded a well-known version of the song "St. Louis
Blues" in 1925, and her starring role in the film yielded the only
known footage of the performer.[1] *Mute* was included in some of
Adkins' performances.

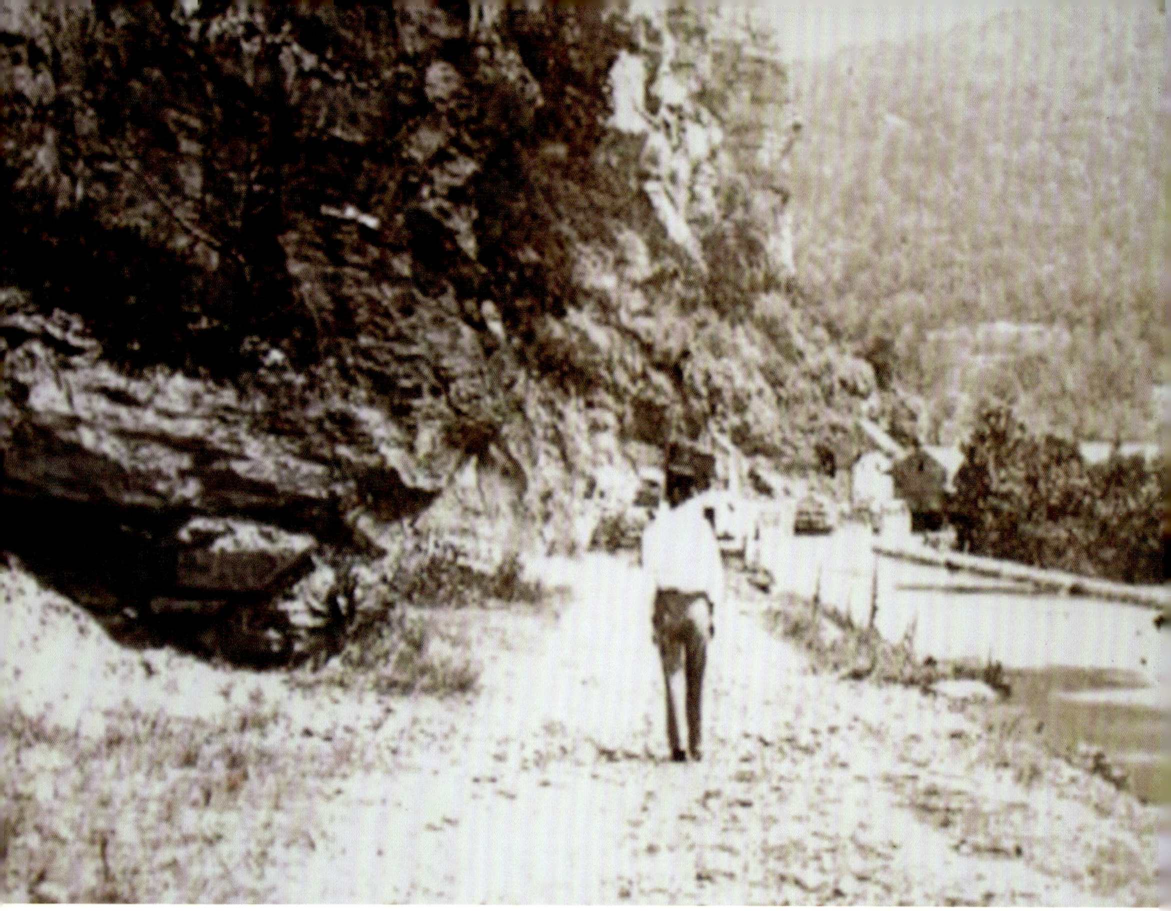

Behold Harpers Ferry

—

2009. Single-channel
stereoscopic digital video,
silent. 10:15 minutes.

—

1. Metcalf, Joel H. and Edward C. Pickering.
"Morehouse's Comet." *Harvard Observatory
Circular* 148 (February 1, 1909): 1–2.

2. Terry Adkins. Email to Joshua Mosley,
October 4, 2009.

Adkins' third video related to abolitionist John Brown, *Behold Harpers Ferry*, was the first for which he employed flickering photographs from scanned stereo cards. The alternating left and right views make each worn, sepia-toned image—of Brown's fort, his grave marker, and the railroad bridge and houses surrounding Harpers Ferry, Virginia, the site of his infamous 1859 raid—silently vibrate with the rapid pulse of life. Adkins also included an image of Comet Morehouse, a comet described as having "no well-defined nucleus which could be used for following in the ordinary way."[1] Adkins, who sometimes noted that he shared a birthday with Brown, used the astronomical image for a break in the video because he wanted "the feeling of the cosmic divine to be there."[2] He was also aware of literature acknowledging Brown, including "The Portent," in which Herman Melville refers to Brown as "the meteor of the war."

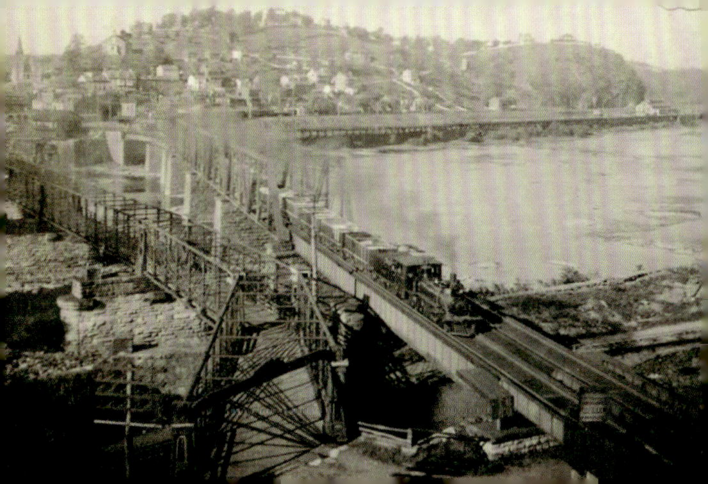

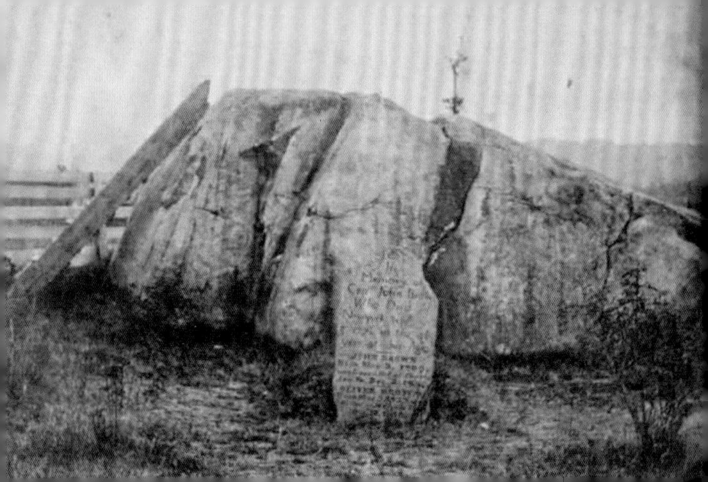

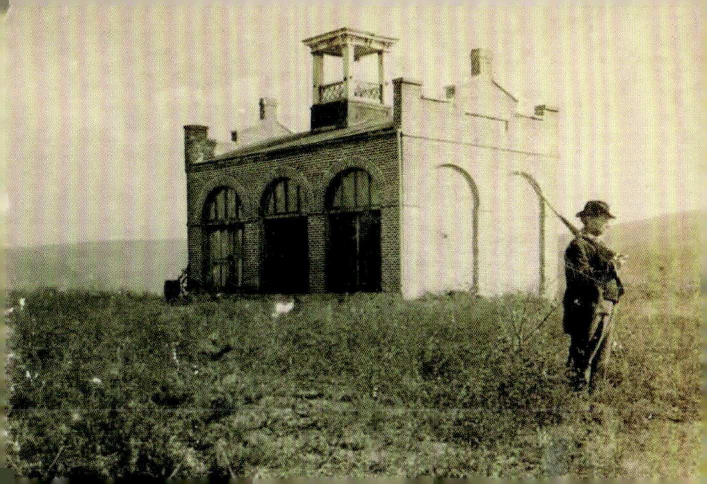

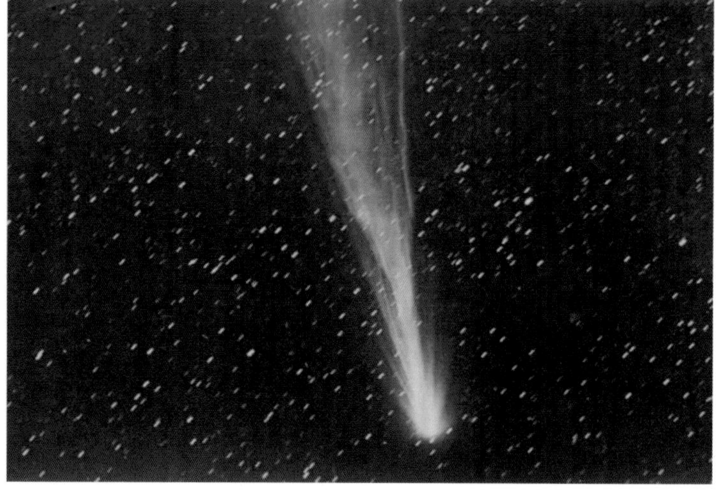

Terry Adkins

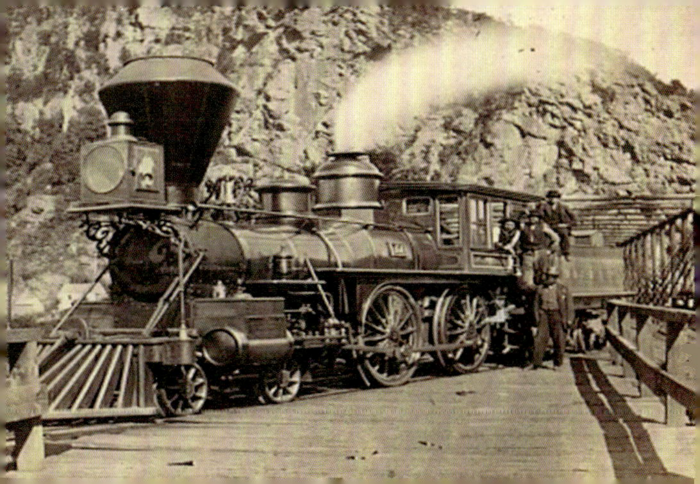

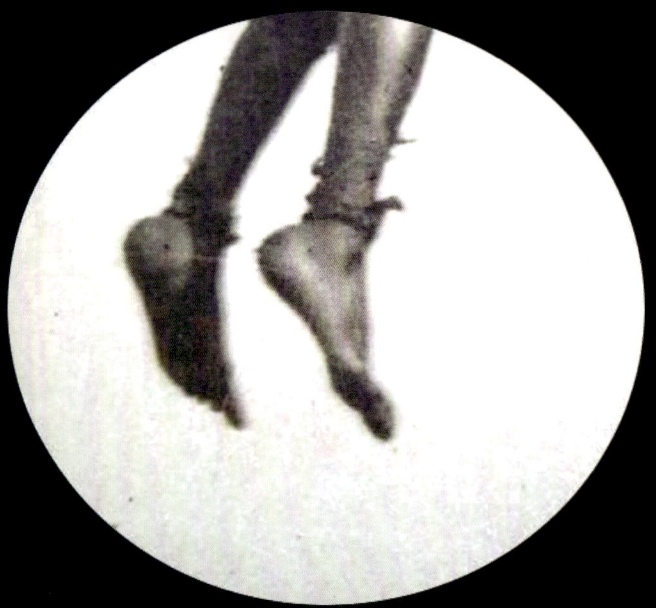

Corpus Specere

—

Circa 2010. Single-channel digital video with sound. 10:45 minutes.

In *Corpus Specere*, horrific black-and-white images of lynched bodies are accompanied by an increasingly layered recitation of the victims' names, towns, death dates, and the accusations against them. When discussing this work, Adkins has cited Ida B. Wells (1862–1931) and W.E.B. Du Bois (1868–1963), fierce anti-lynching activists who were among the founding members of the NAACP. Adkins incorporated this video into multiple Lone Wolf Recital Corps performances, including: *Corpus Specere* at the Romanian Academy in Rome in 2010; *Facets: A Recital Compilation* at the Frances Young Tang Teaching Museum and Art Gallery in conjunction with his thirty-year retrospective in 2012; and *Postlude (Corpus Specere)* at The Studio Museum in Harlem in conjunction with *Radical Presence: Black Performance in Contemporary Art* in 2013.

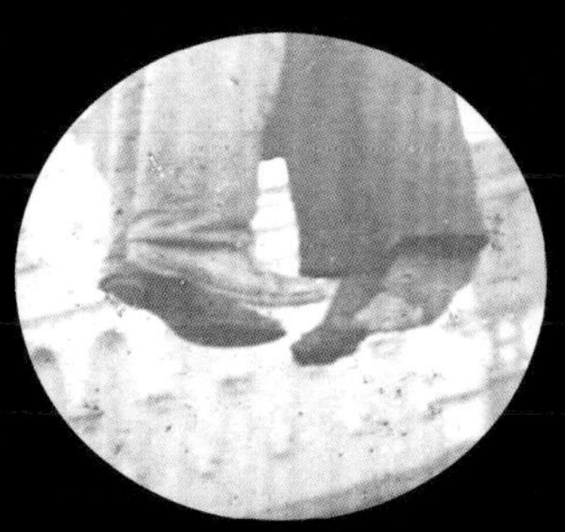

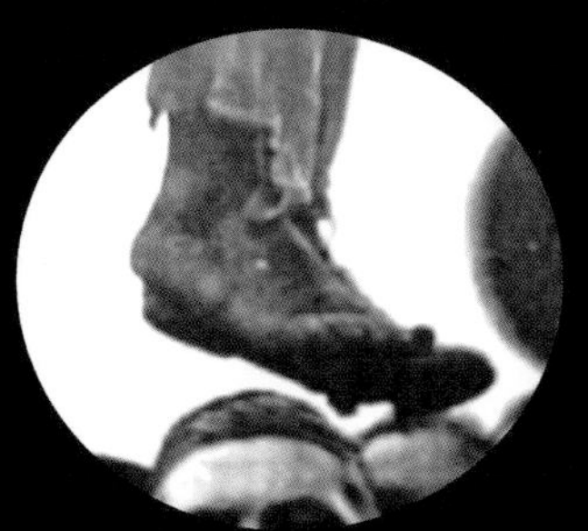

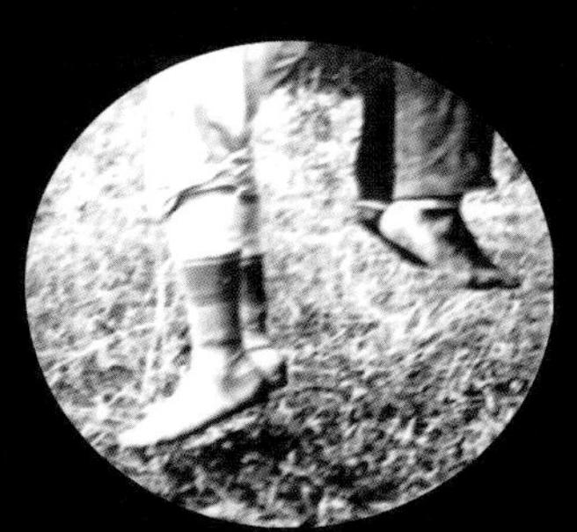

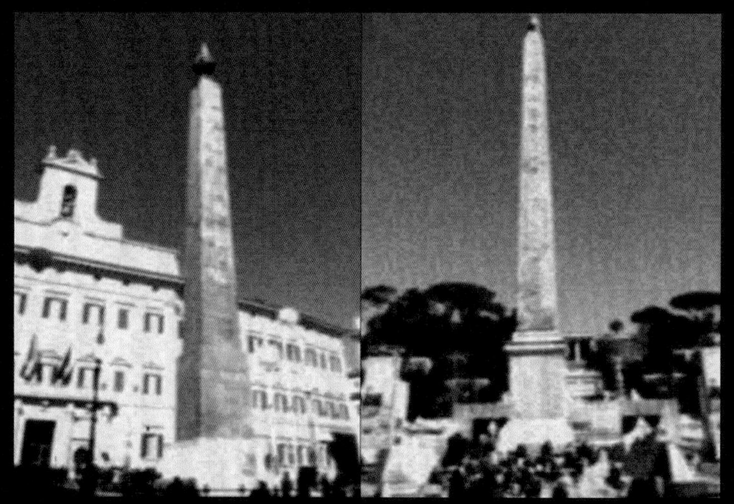

Obelisks in Rome

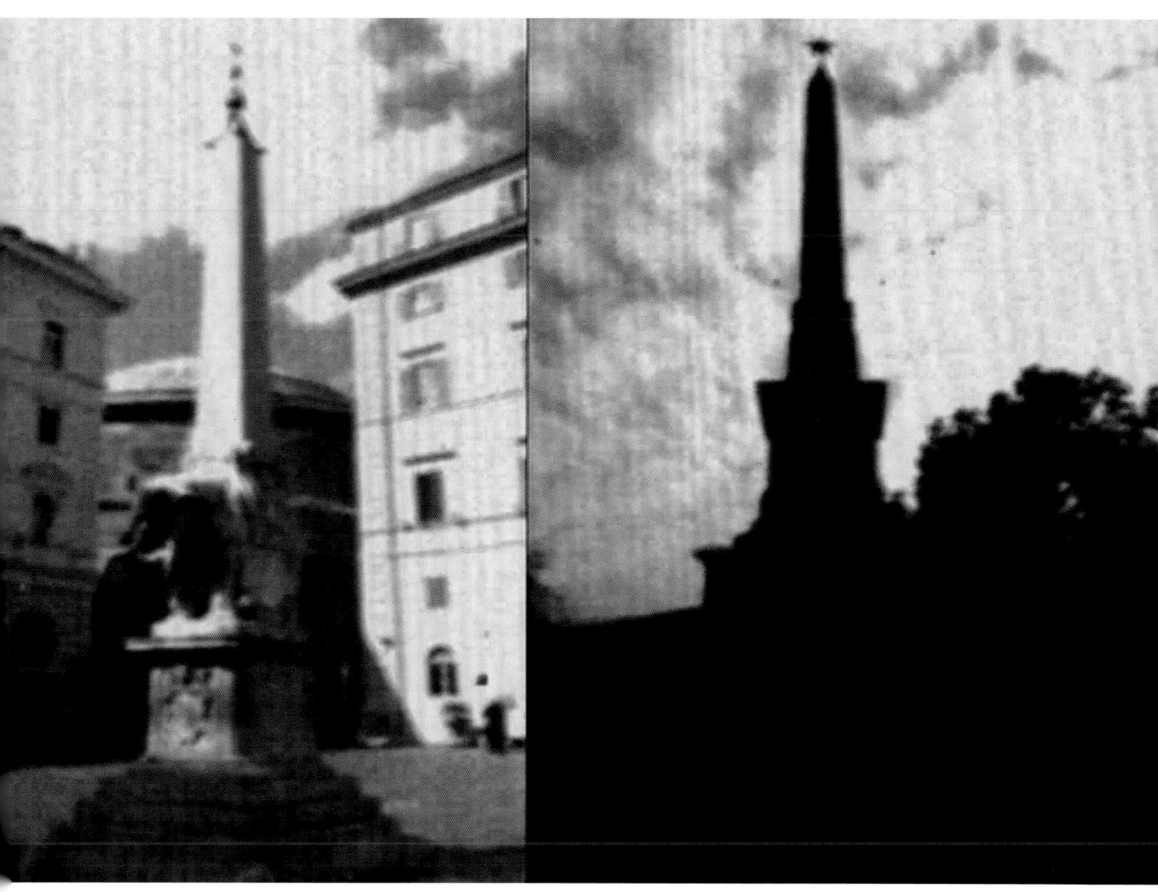

2012. Single-channel digital
video, silent. 46:10 minutes.

1. For more information on the Egyptian
obelisks in Rome, see Susan Sorek's 2010
book, *The Emperors' Needles: Egyptian
Obelisks and Rome.*

2. The Studio Museum in Harlem, "Terry
Adkins, Blanche Bruce, and the Lone
Wolf Recital Corps: At Osiris (2013)," 2013,
accessed on January 5, 2016. https://www.
youtube.com/watch?v=Lyhzys9nH-U

Obelisks in Rome offers split-screen, grainy black-
and-white views of the ancient Egyptian obelisks
that were removed from their places of origin and
erected throughout the Italian city, where they were
often adorned with symbols related to Christianity.[1]
This silent video was projected during *At Osiris*—a
2013 performance at The Studio Museum in Harlem,
held in conjunction with *Radical Presence: Black
Performance in Contemporary Art*—while Adkins and
members of the Lone Wolf Recital Corps played
instruments and recited segments of "ancient
Egyptian Osirian texts."[2] Adkins, who was a Fellow at
the American Academy in Rome, traveled to Rome
several times for exhibitions and performances.

Dante Paradiso XXVII

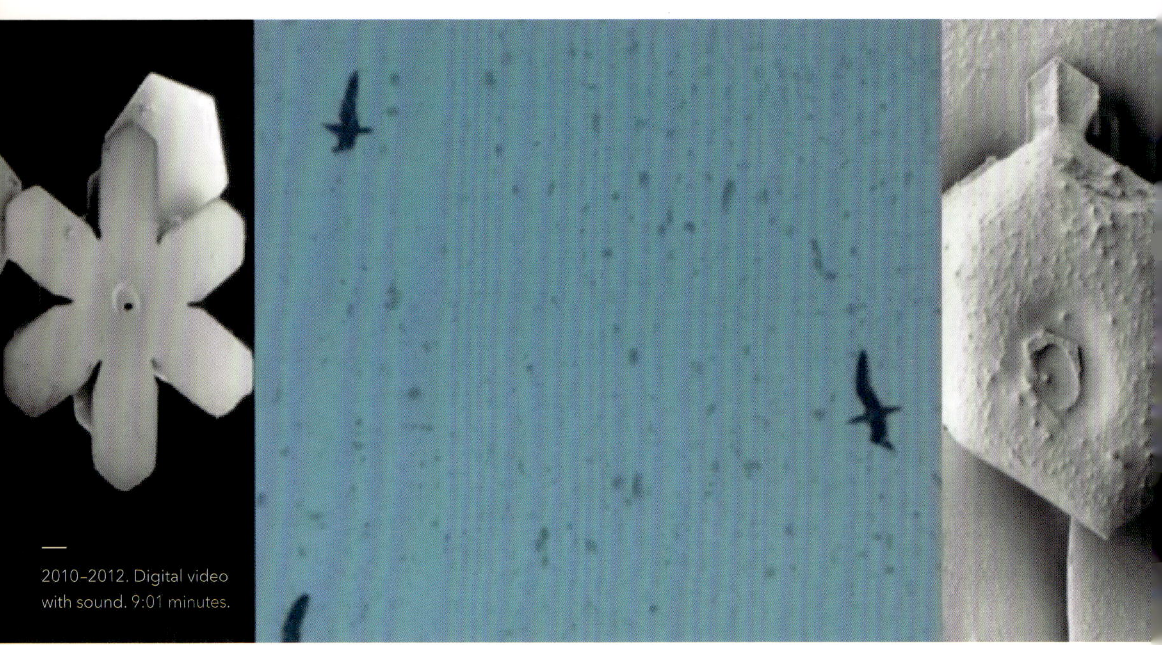

2010–2012. Digital video with sound. 9:01 minutes.

Dante Paradiso XXVII is a split-screen video that refers to *The Divine Comedy: The Vision of Paradise, Purgatory, and Hell*, written by Italian poet and philosopher Dante Alighieri (1265–1321).[1] Allen Mandelbaum's translation of Dante's "Paradiso—Canto XXVII" includes the lines:

> *As, when the horn of heaven's Goat abuts*
> *the sun, our sky flakes frozen vapors downward,*
> *so did I see that ether there adorned;*
>
> *for from that sphere, triumphant vapors now*
> *were flaking up to the Empyrean-*
> *returning after dwelling here with us.*

The video's center section shows inverted footage of snow falling outside Adkins' window in Rome, while the left and right sections alternate between various stereo card images of microscopic views of snowflakes (similar to his *Miy Paluk 1866*). The soundtrack is comprised of a voiceover by Adkins and a female narrator reading "Canto XXVII" simultaneously in English and Italian, respectively, while music filters in and a fire seems to crackle nearby. Are cold snowflakes falling down or are hot ashes rising up? Occasionally, a bird gently glides through the frame, perhaps to reference spirits.

Adkins said that after his father died, he looked "to bodies of literature that would make real for [him] the fact that [he] would someday see him again," including Dante's "Paradiso" and the book of Revelation.[2] Adkins incorporated *Dante Paradiso XXVII* into multiple performances, including *Paradiso XXVII* at the Romanian Academy in Rome in 2010 and *Facets: A Recital Compilation* at the Tang Museum in 2012.

---

1. In another version, Adkins used only the blue center segment of the video, and the soundtrack excluded the reading of "Canto XXVII."

2. Adkins, Terry and George Lewis. "Event Scores: Terry Adkins and George Lewis in Conversation." *Artforum International*, March 2014, 244–253.

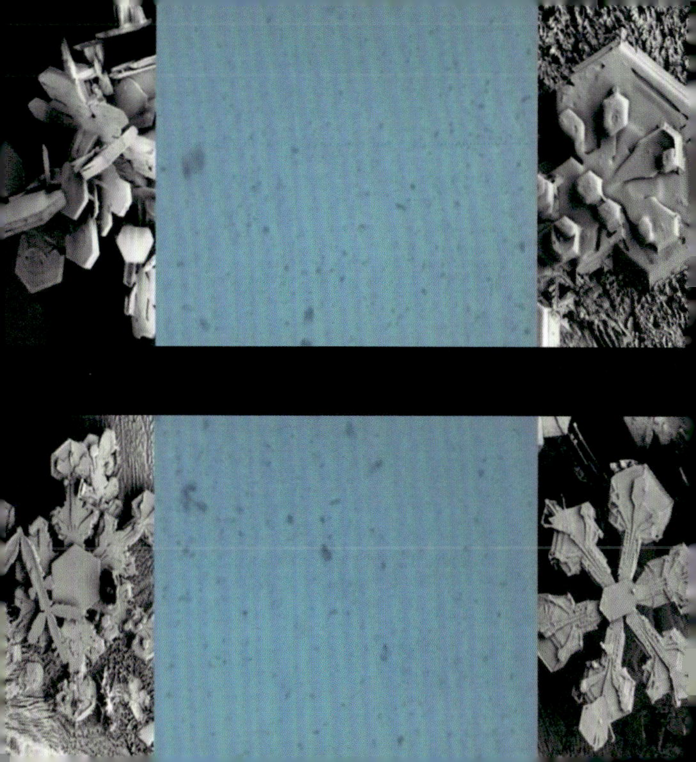

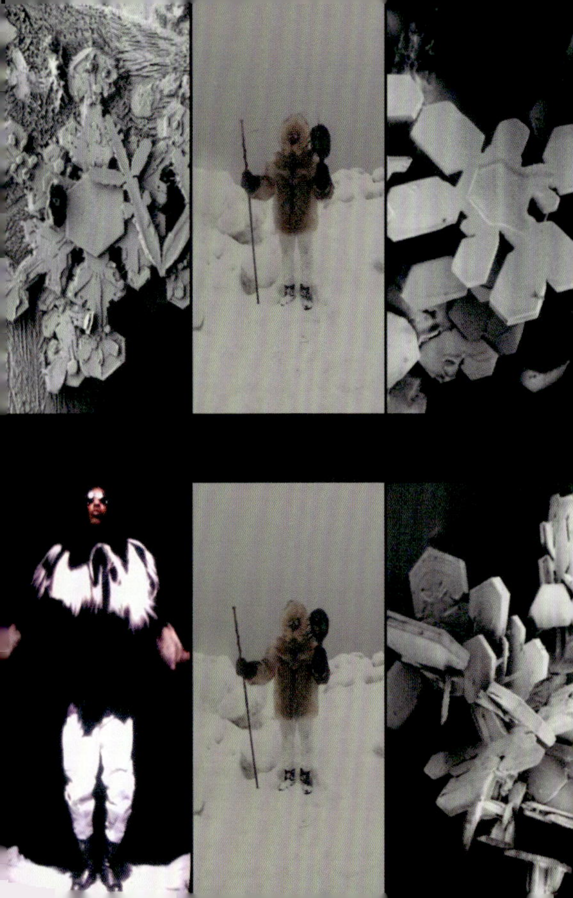

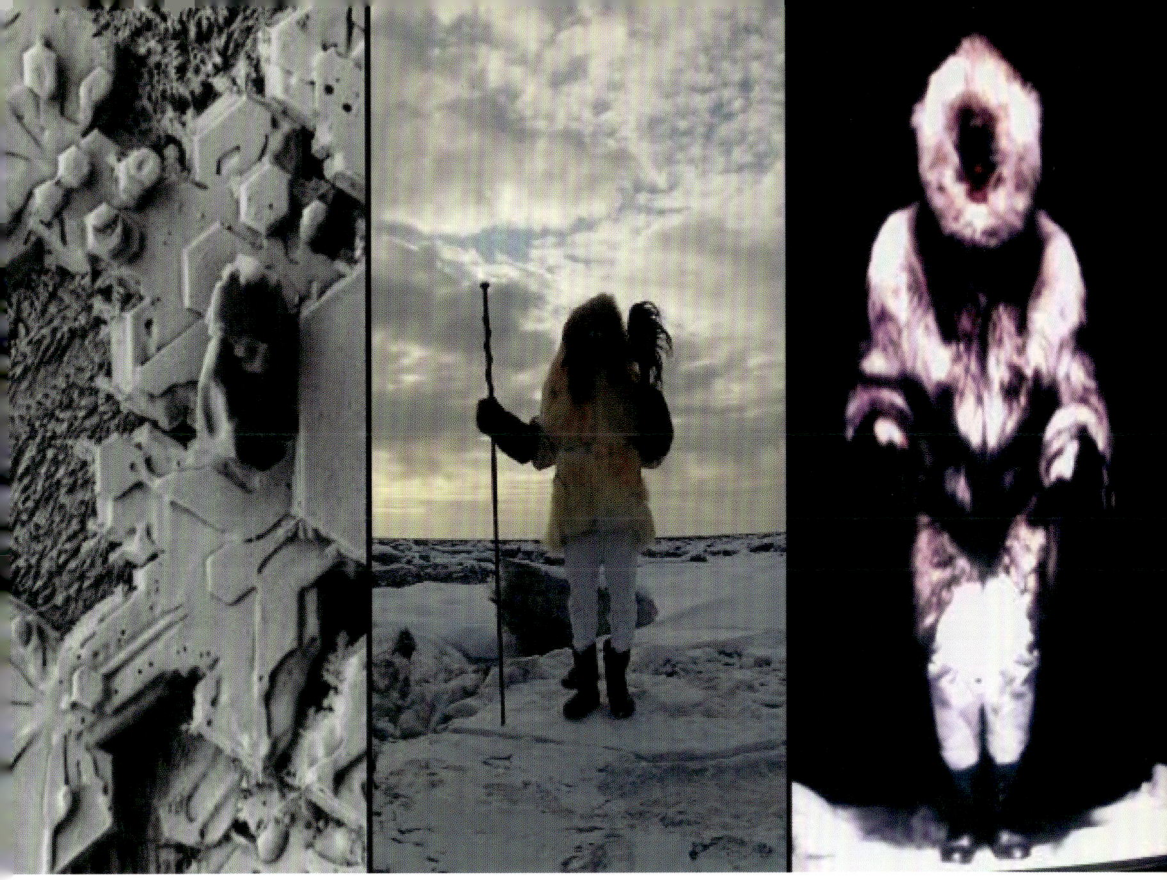

Miy Paluk 1866

—

2012. Single-channel digital video with sound (originally presented as a three-channel video on monitors). 24:26 minutes.

Miy Paluk 1866 is a split-screen video that celebrates Matthew Henson, the first African-American Arctic explorer and a member of Robert Peary's polar expeditionary team. Contrary to popular belief, Henson (1866–1955) was co-discoverer of the Geographic North Pole in 1909, and was arguably the first person to reach the Pole. He also became a member of the surrounding Inuit community, learning their language, trades, and customs (they called him "Miy Paluk," which means "Matthew, the Kind One").

Dressed in furs and shown both standing motionless (as in his 2001 *Roost* video) and jumping in slow-motion, Adkins embodies the dual spirit of Henson / Miy Paluk. The animated microscopic stereo images of snow reference both the historical figure and the destination.[1] Regarding his sculptures, photographs, and videos that address Henson, Adkins wrote that his "primary objectives" were to "recast [Henson's] artisanal skills as those of an artist proper and to reconsider his entire Arctic enterprise as a magnum opus of immersive artistic research."[2]

1. Gaines, Charles. "Chanting Bees and Other Translations: The Video Projects of Terry Adkins." In *Terry Adkins: Recital*, edited by Ian Berry. Prestel (forthcoming).

2. Adkins, Terry. "Nutjuitok (Polar Star) After Matthew Henson." *Le Journal de la Triennale* 5 (2012): 22.

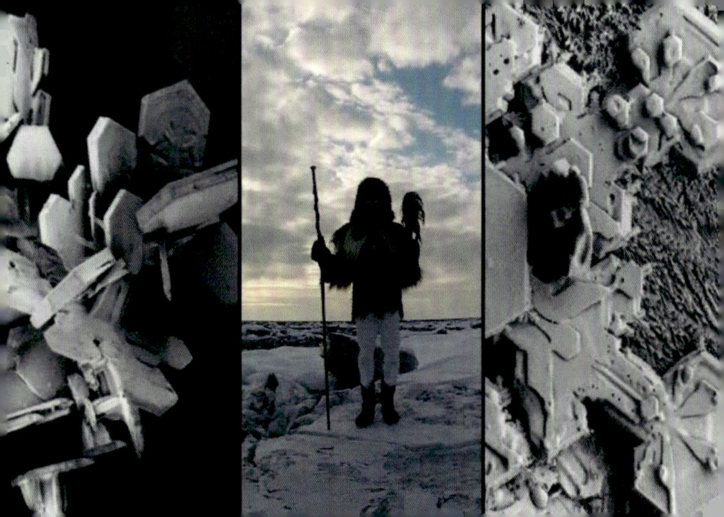

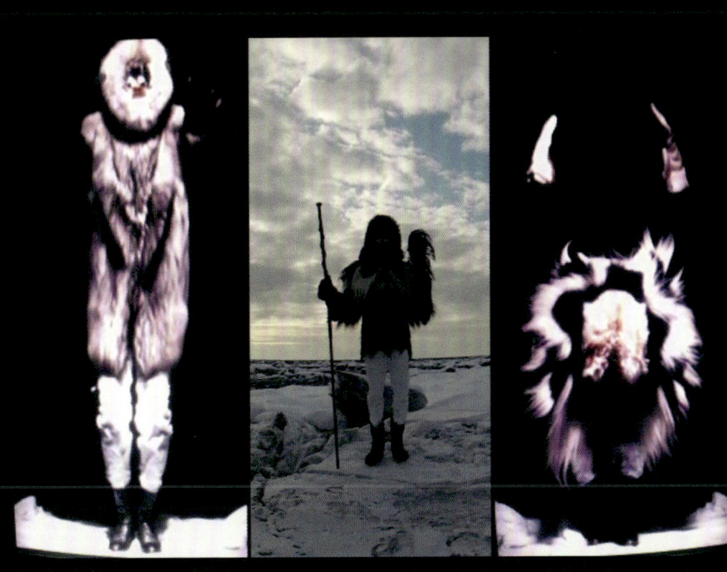

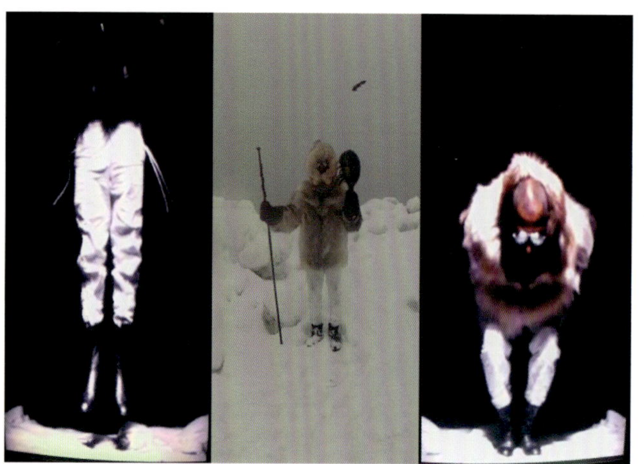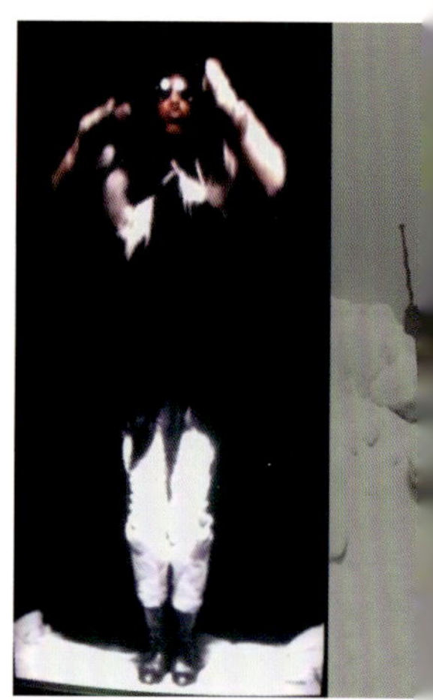

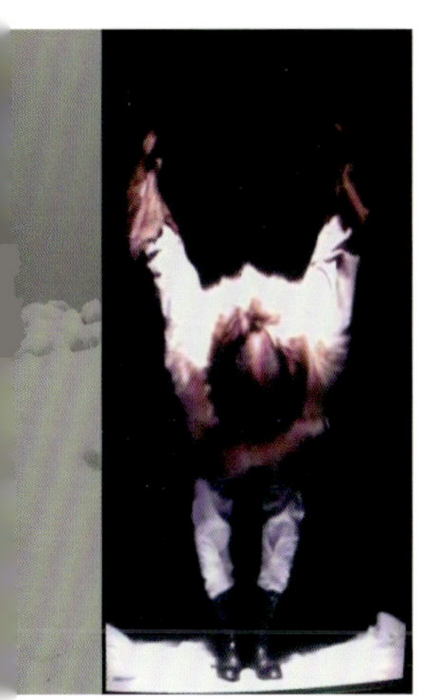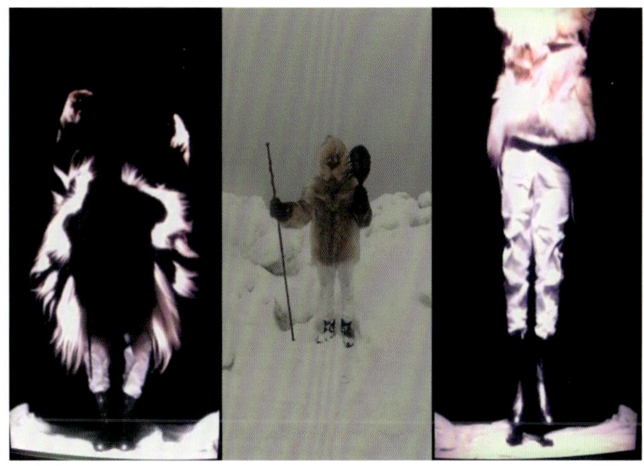

Nutjuitok II

2012. Single-channel digital video with sound. 17:00 minutes.

For the images in Adkins' photographic series *Nutjuitok (Polar Star) After Matthew Henson 1866*, maps of the North Pole and surrounding regions were projected onto the artist's body, which was adorned with furs as he held implements related to trade and exploration. Adkins wrote that "the symmetry in the *Miy Paluk* video and *Nutjuitok* photographic suite symbolizes an attempt to harness the centrality and magnetism of the polar axis itself."[1]

For Adkins' video *Nutjuitok II*, he made a slideshow of his *Nutjuitok (Polar Star)* photographs and set them to a soundtrack that echoes the mysterious electronic hissing and chirping and extended percussive notes in *Miy Paluk 1866*. The soundtrack also includes layers of voices, which are probably speaking and singing in Inuktitut, the language of the Inuit community that welcomed Henson. Adkins, who wanted to "create sound works influenced by native drum music, throat singing, dance and storytelling," said that he would employ Inuktitut and English in his performances and videos as a "harnessing device of Henson's imagination and the enriching insular experience that Inuit culture afforded him through language."[2] *Nutjuitok II* was included in some of Adkins' performances.

1. Adkins, Terry. "Nutjuitok (Polar Star) After Matthew Henson." *Le Journal de la Triennale* 5 (2012): 22.

2. Adkins, Terry. Miy Paluk (Ahdoolo). Unpublished residency proposal, 2011.

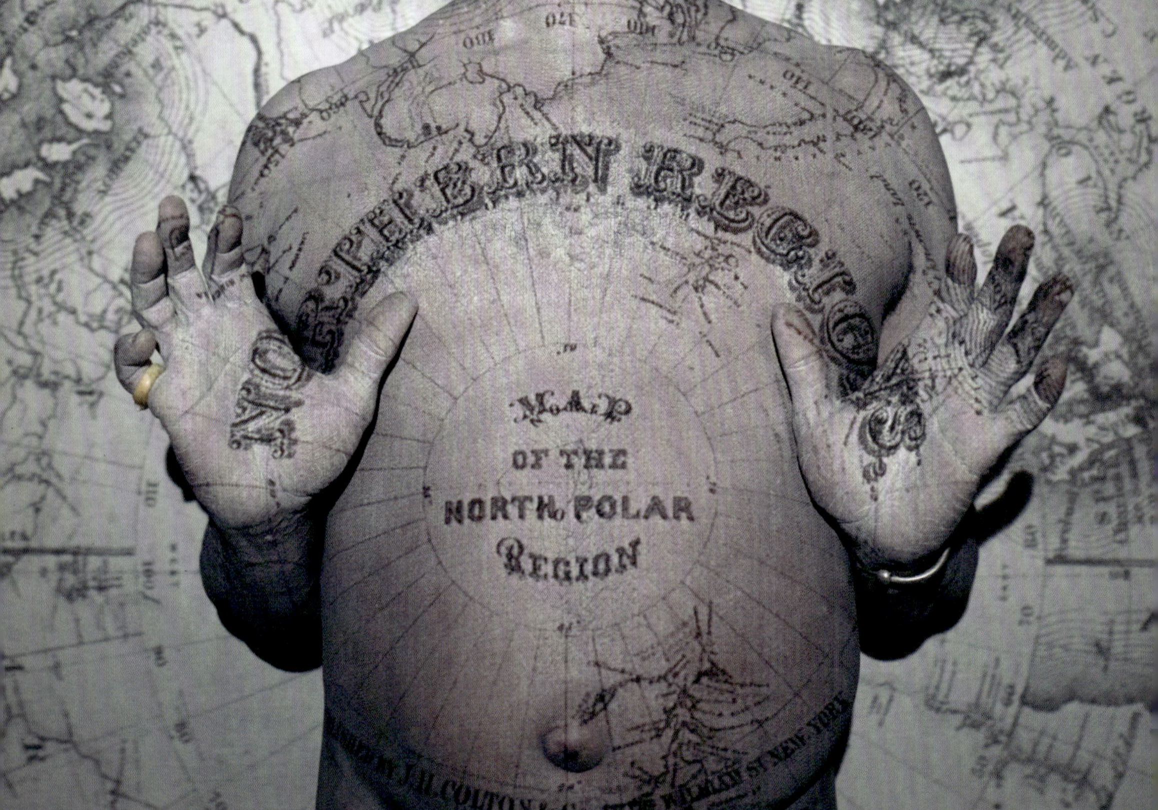

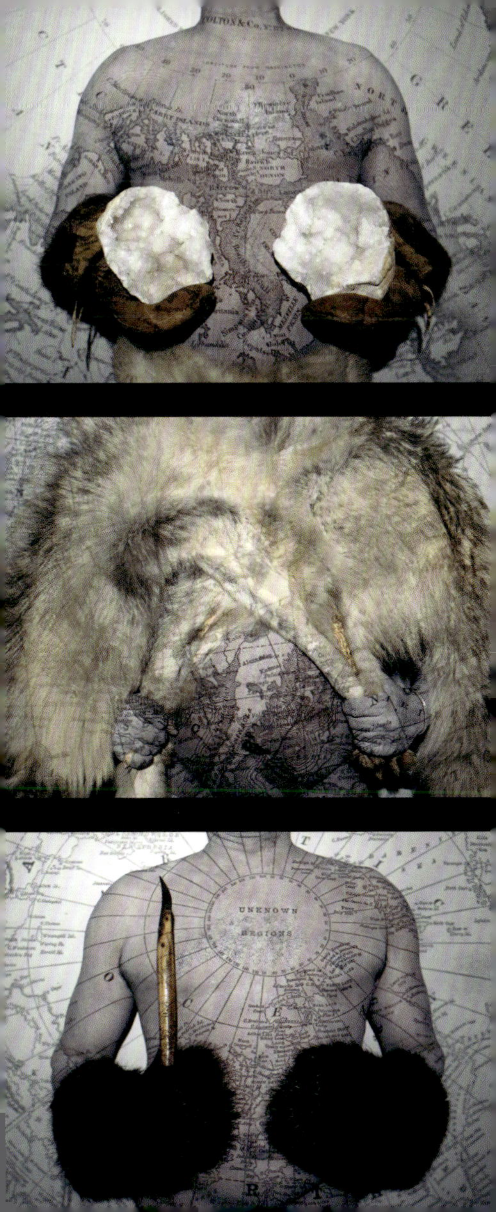
UNKNOWN
REGIONS

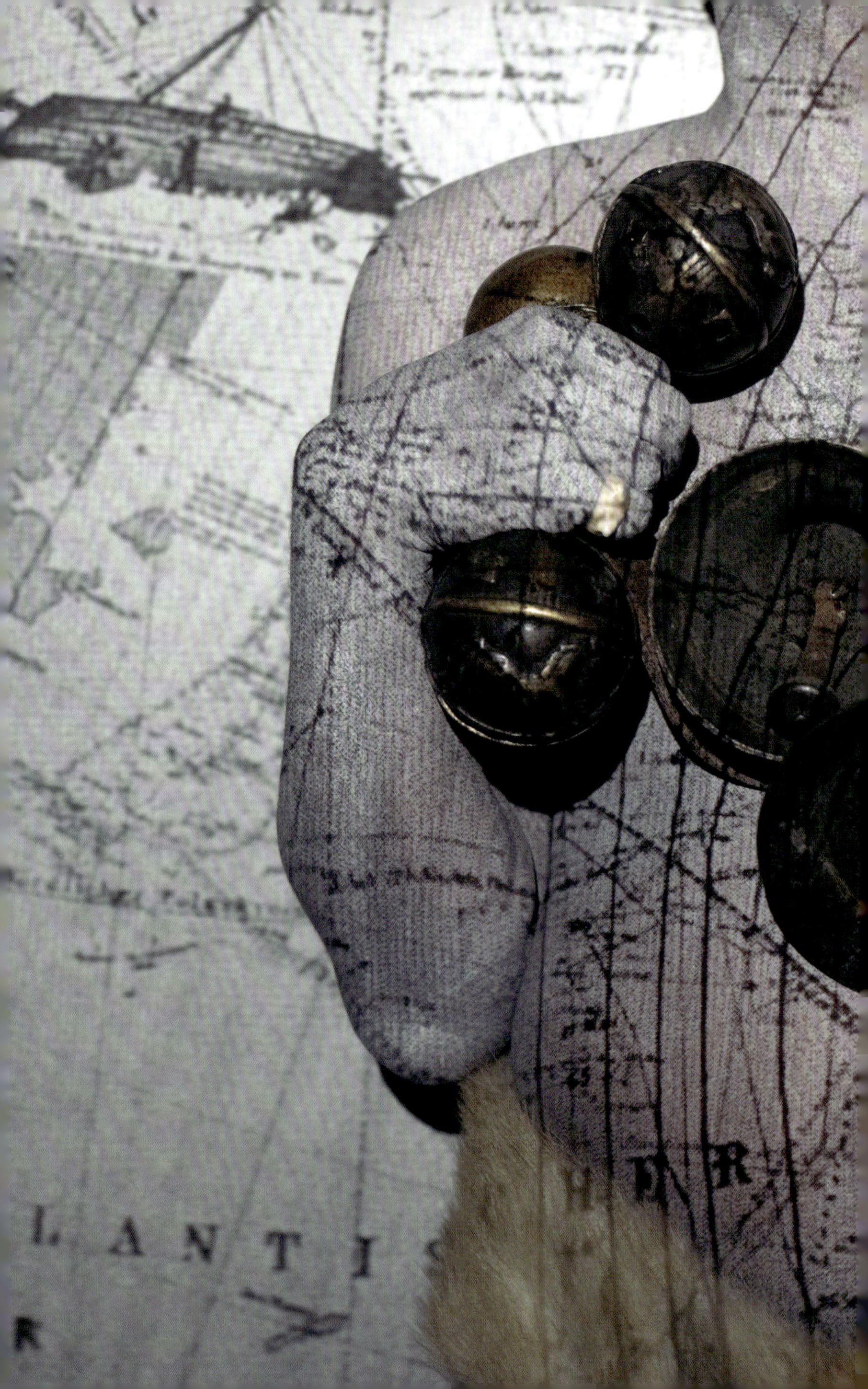

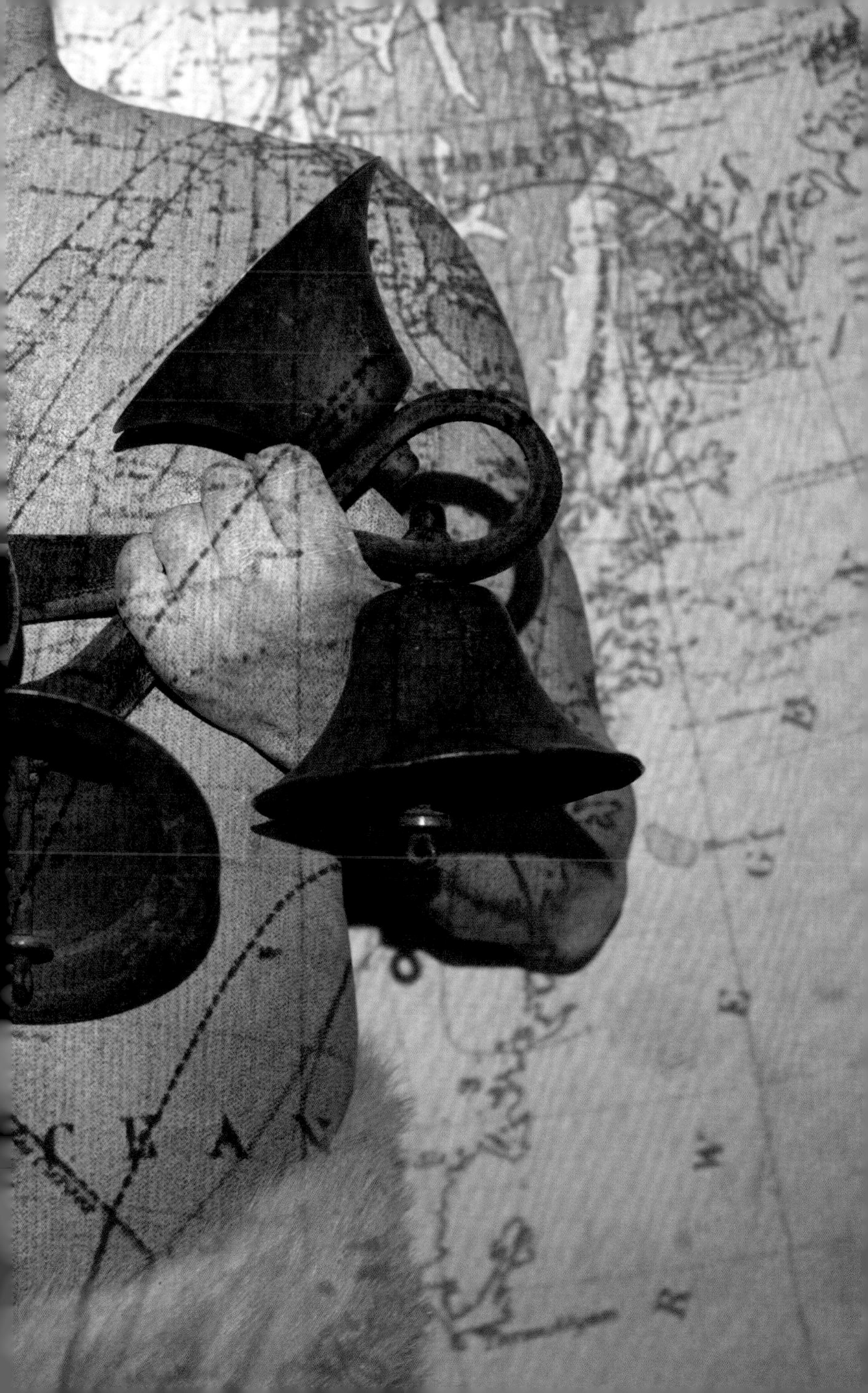

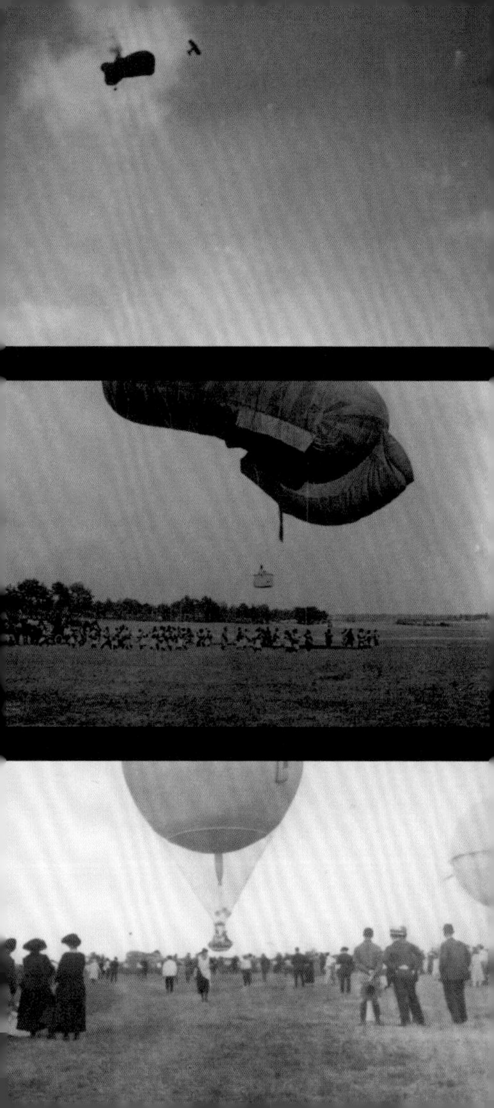

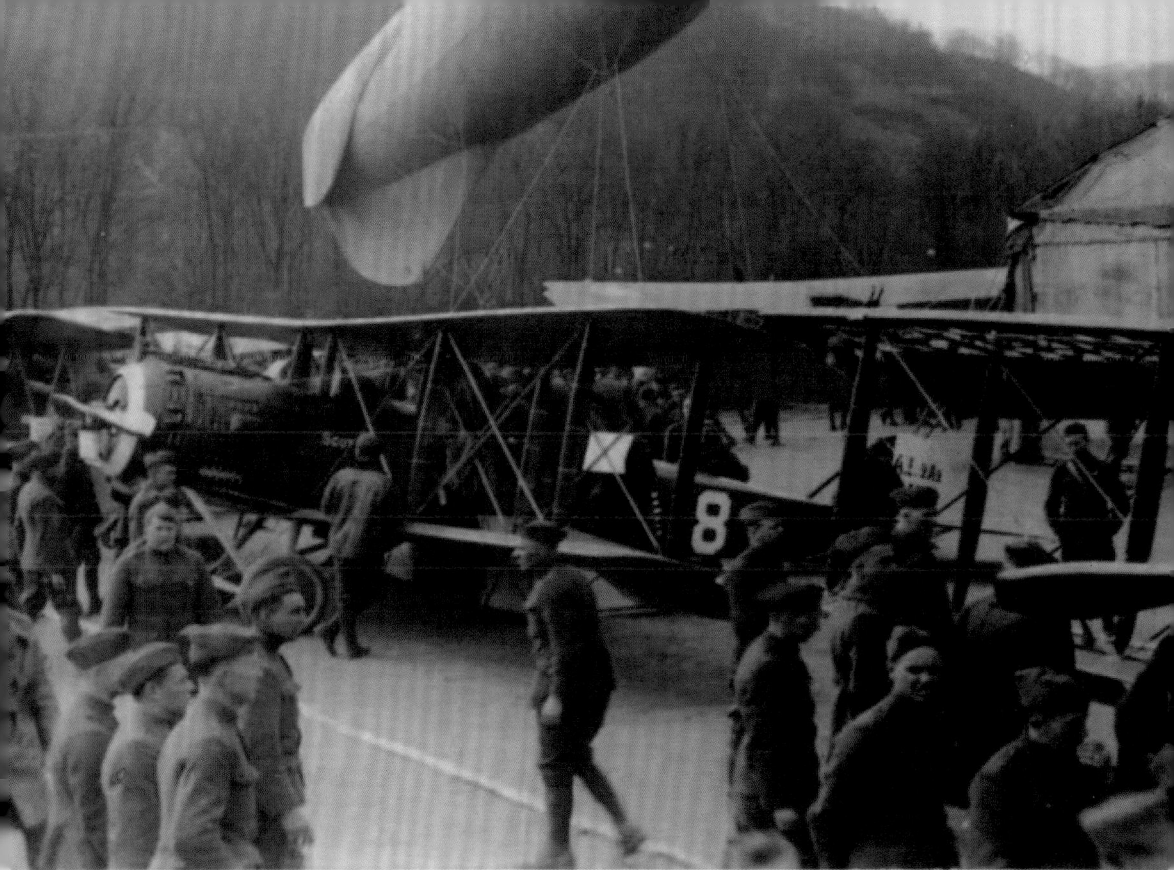

Flumen Orationis
(from The Principalities)

2012. Single-channel
stereoscopic digital video
with sound. 41:37 minutes.

1. Adkins, Terry. "Terry Adkins:
Recital." Interview by Ian Berry.
The Tang Museum (2012). Available
at https://vimeo.com/49853092.

For *Flumen Orationis*, Adkins overlaid Martin Luther King Jr.'s 1967 "Why I Am Opposed to the War in Vietnam" speech with Jimi Hendrix's 1970 protest song "Machine Gun." Adkins said that Hendrix (1942–1970) and King (1929–1968) both "came into [his] life at the same time" and that pairing them was a "very natural thing" because there was "no greater pacifist plea" than King's address and "no greater pacifist rallying cry" than Hendrix's song.[1] The powerful soundtrack is accompanied by flickering black-and-white images (from scanned stereo cards) of early manned flight—dirigibles, hot air balloons, and planes—to reference Hendrix's little-discussed time as a paratrooper in the 101st Airborne Division of the U.S. Army.

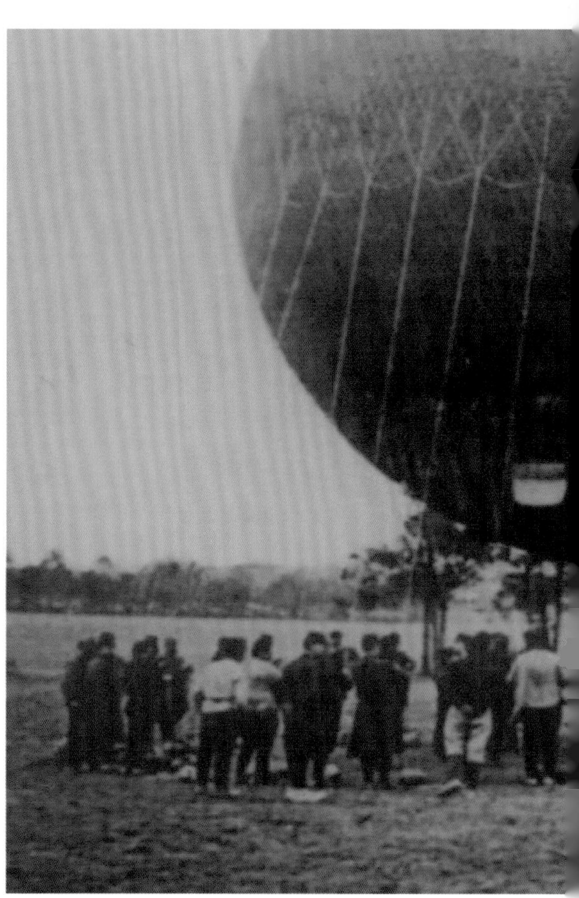

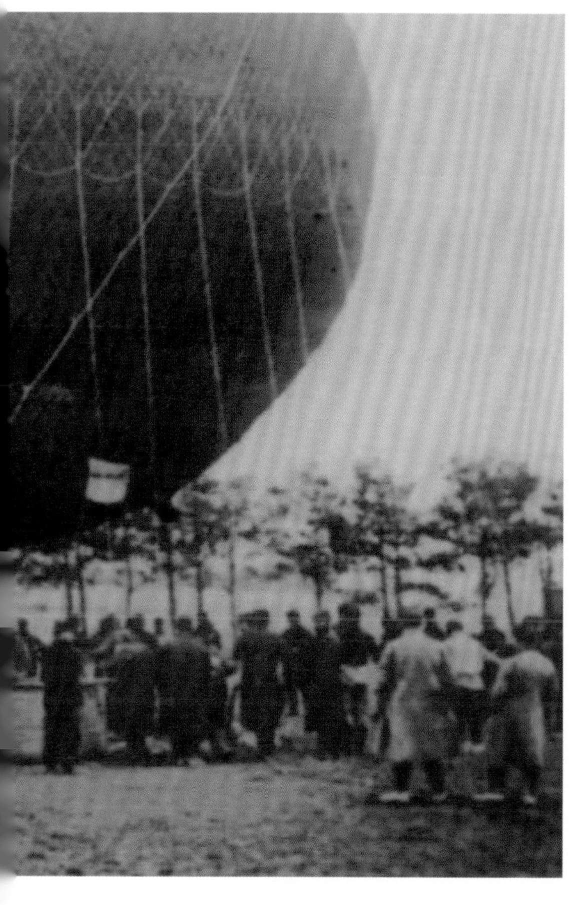

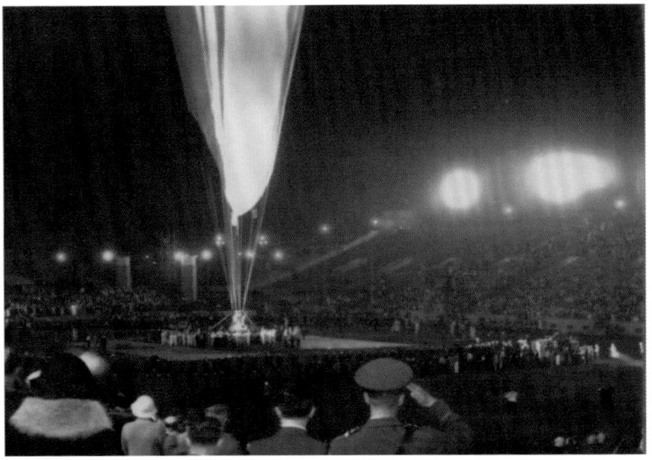

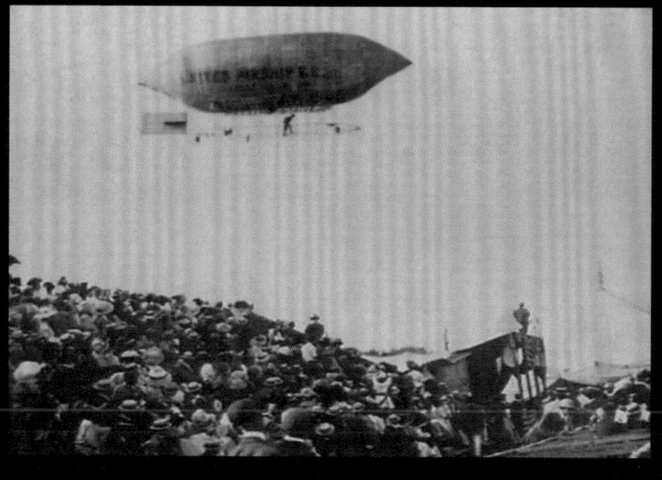

Flumen Orationis (from The Principalities)

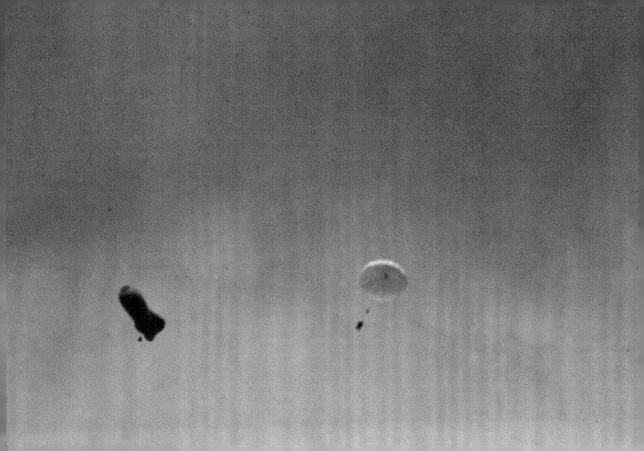

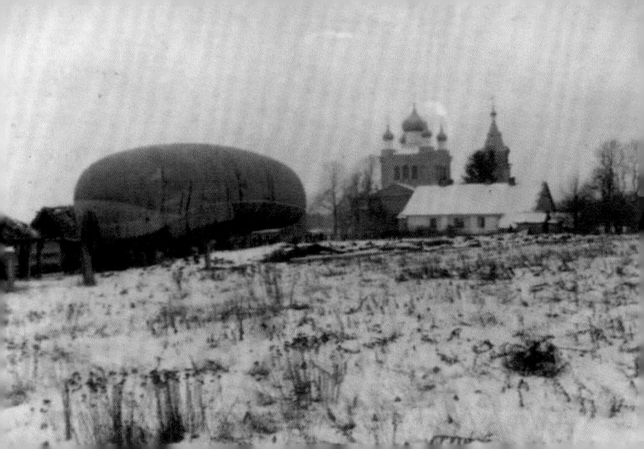

Glorioso (from Nenuphar)

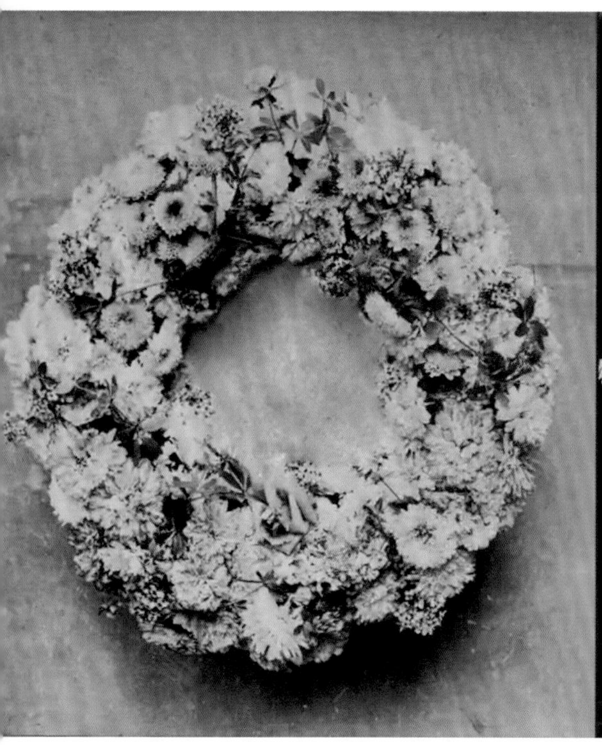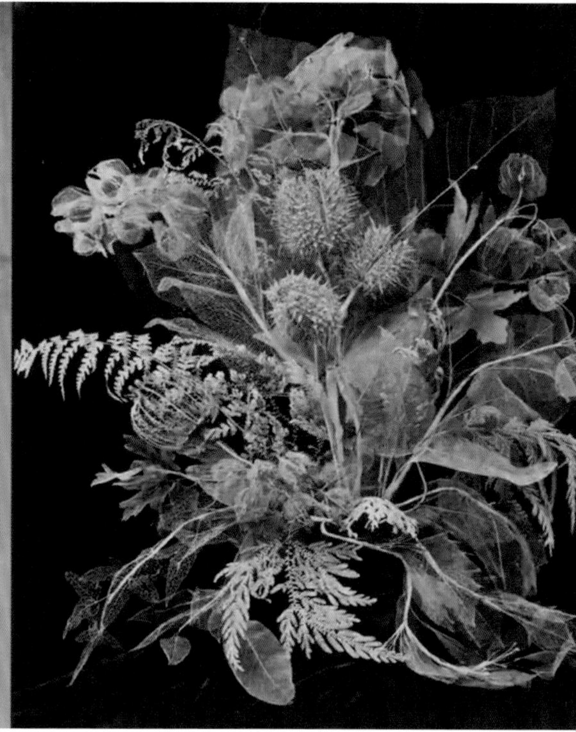

2013. Single-channel
stereoscopic digital video,
silent. 26:10 minutes.

Glorioso (from Nenuphar) is a silent digital video featuring split-screen black-and-white stereo images of memorial wreaths and bouquets. Other than the opening widescreen view of a wreath, the gently pulsating images of floral-draped crosses, rose-covered anchors, droopy flowering bushes, and elegant leafy arrangements are paired with their mirror image, a different floral arrangement, or a black screen.

This video was exhibited in *Nenuphar*, Adkins' 2013 exhibition at Salon 94, New York. The collection of works he created for the project addresses unfamiliar, and sometimes fictional, connections between the legacies of botanist and inventor George Washington Carver (1864–1943) and artist Yves Klein (1928–1962), including references to "botany, agriculture, nautica, religion, music, and ancient Egypt."[1] For the exhibition, Adkins also repurposed the back sides of these stereo cards to make his *Progressive Nature Studies*, a printed "fake folio of what are supposed to be George Washington Carver paintings," to allude to *Peintures*, Klein's portfolio of non-existent monochrome paintings.[2]

1. Salon 94. "Terry Adkins: Nenuphar," press release, October 2013.

2. Adkins, Terry. "Interview with Terry Adkins." By Jessica Slaven. *Paper Monument: A Journal of Contemporary Art* (2013).

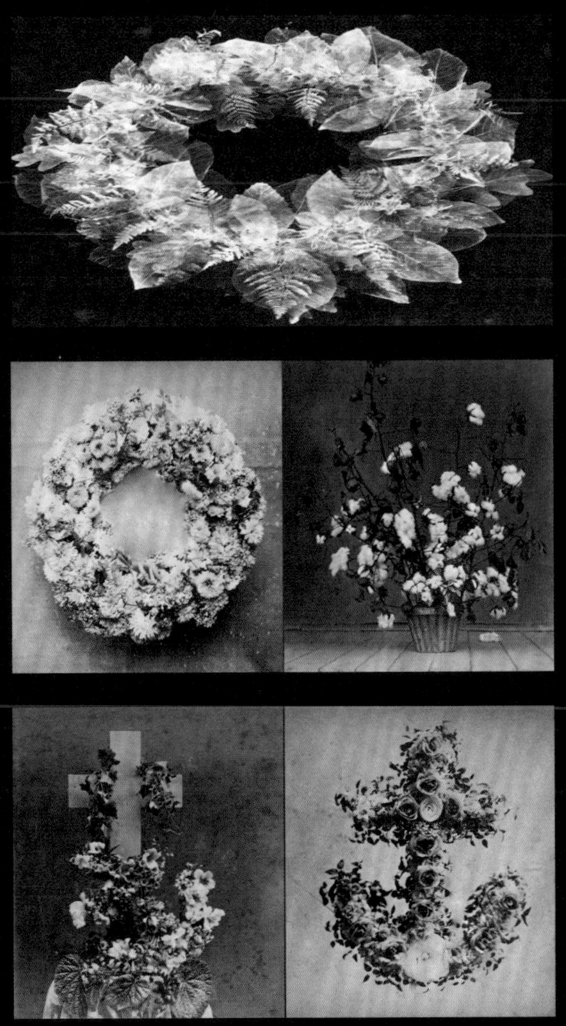

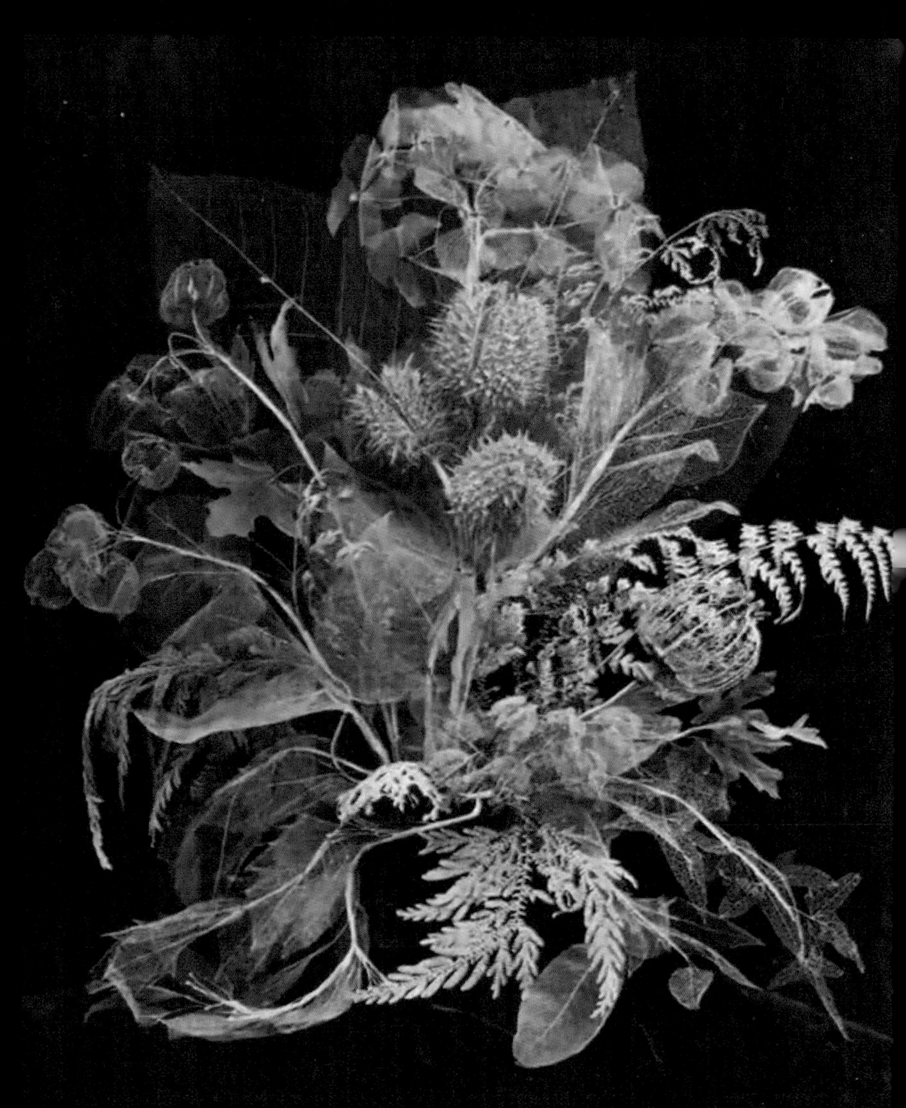

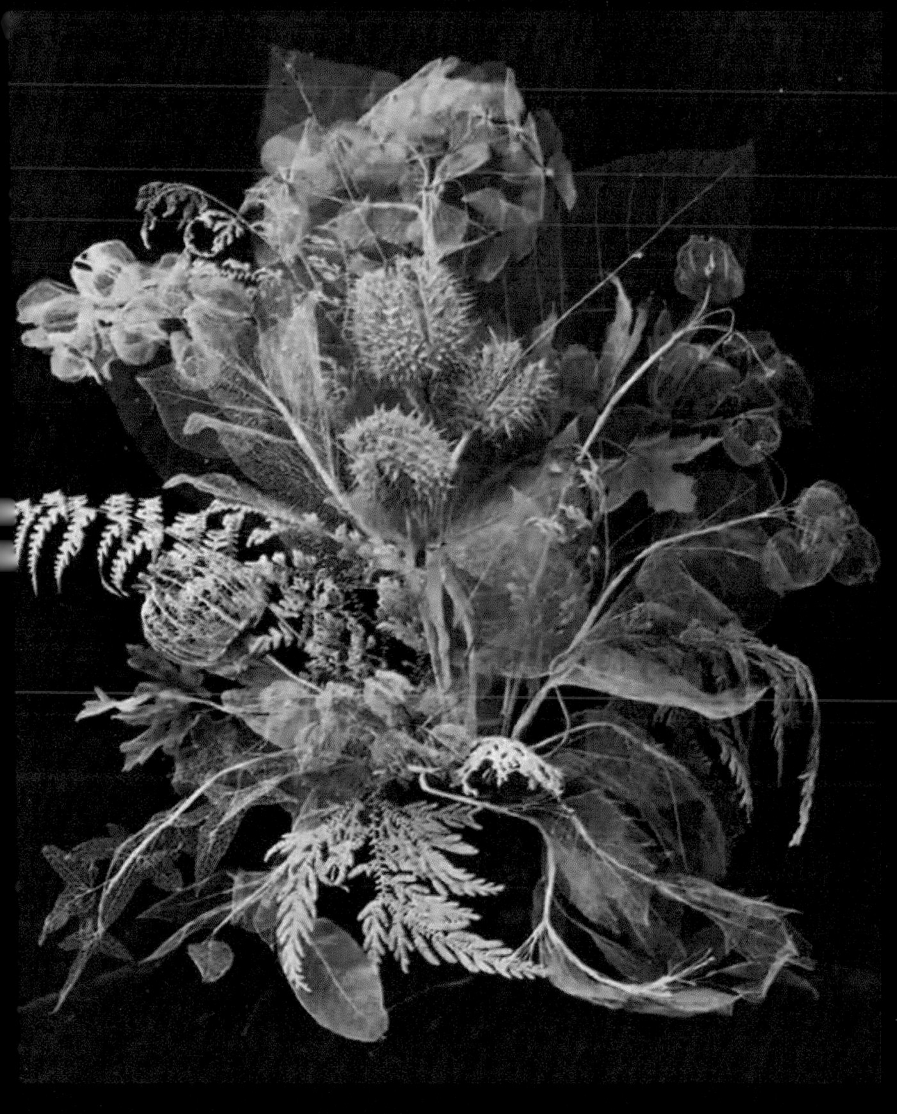

Glorioso (from Nenuphar)

TERRY ADKINS

SOLDIER SHEPHERD PROPHET MARTYR

Videos from 1998–2013

This exhibition has been made possible by a grant from The Andy Warhol Foundation for the Visual Arts, with additional funding from the Illinois Arts Council Agency.

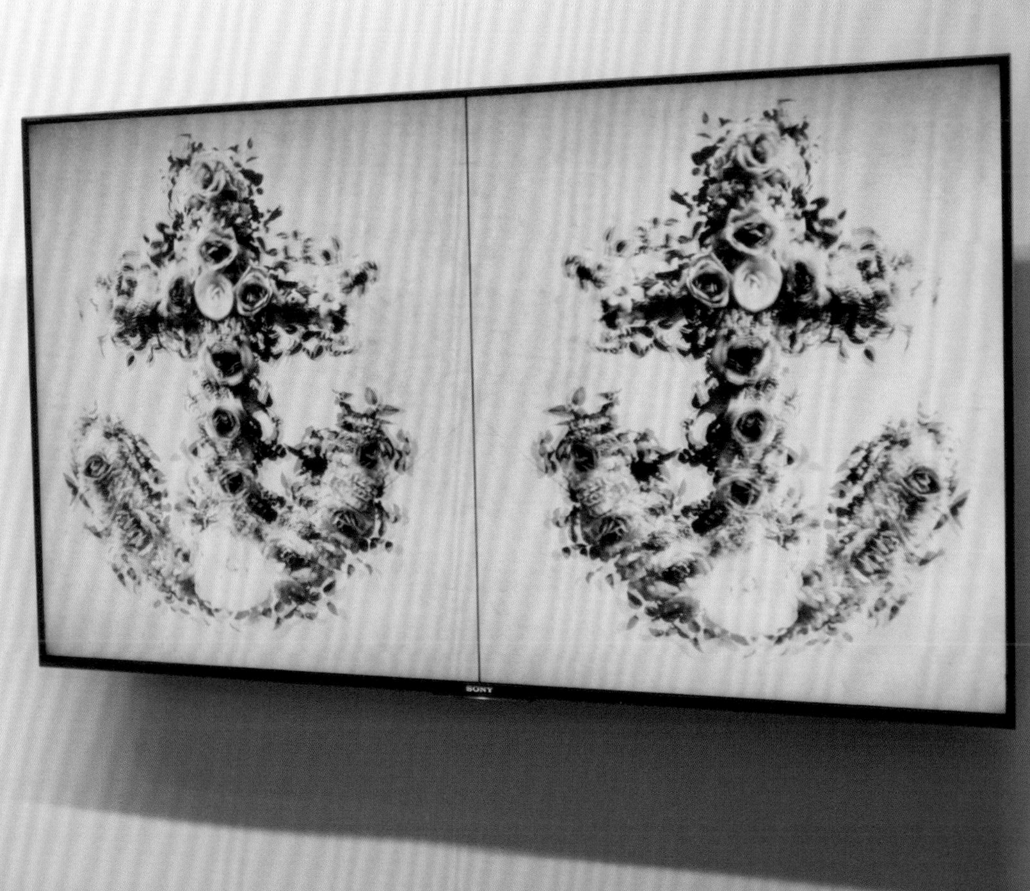
SONY

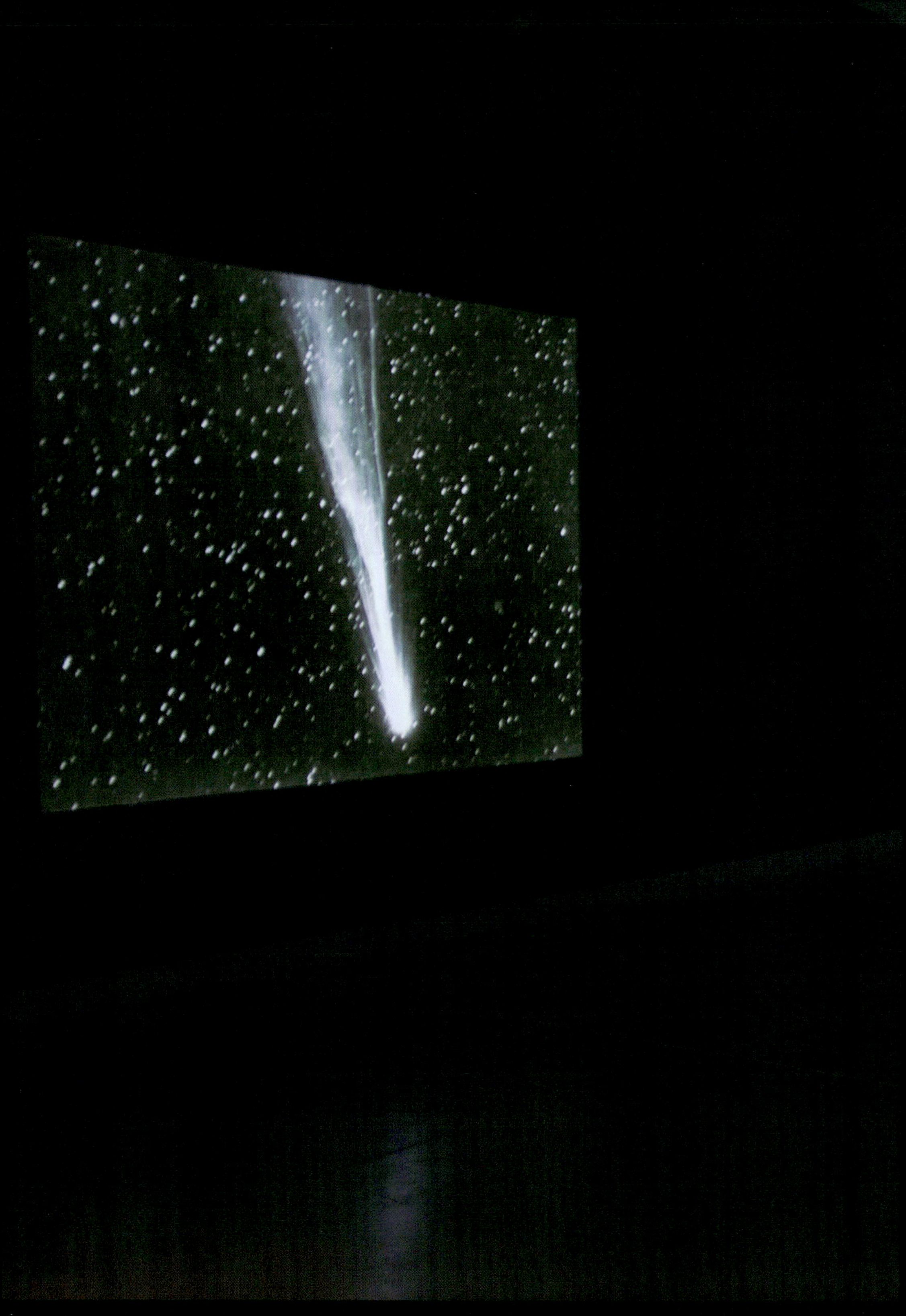

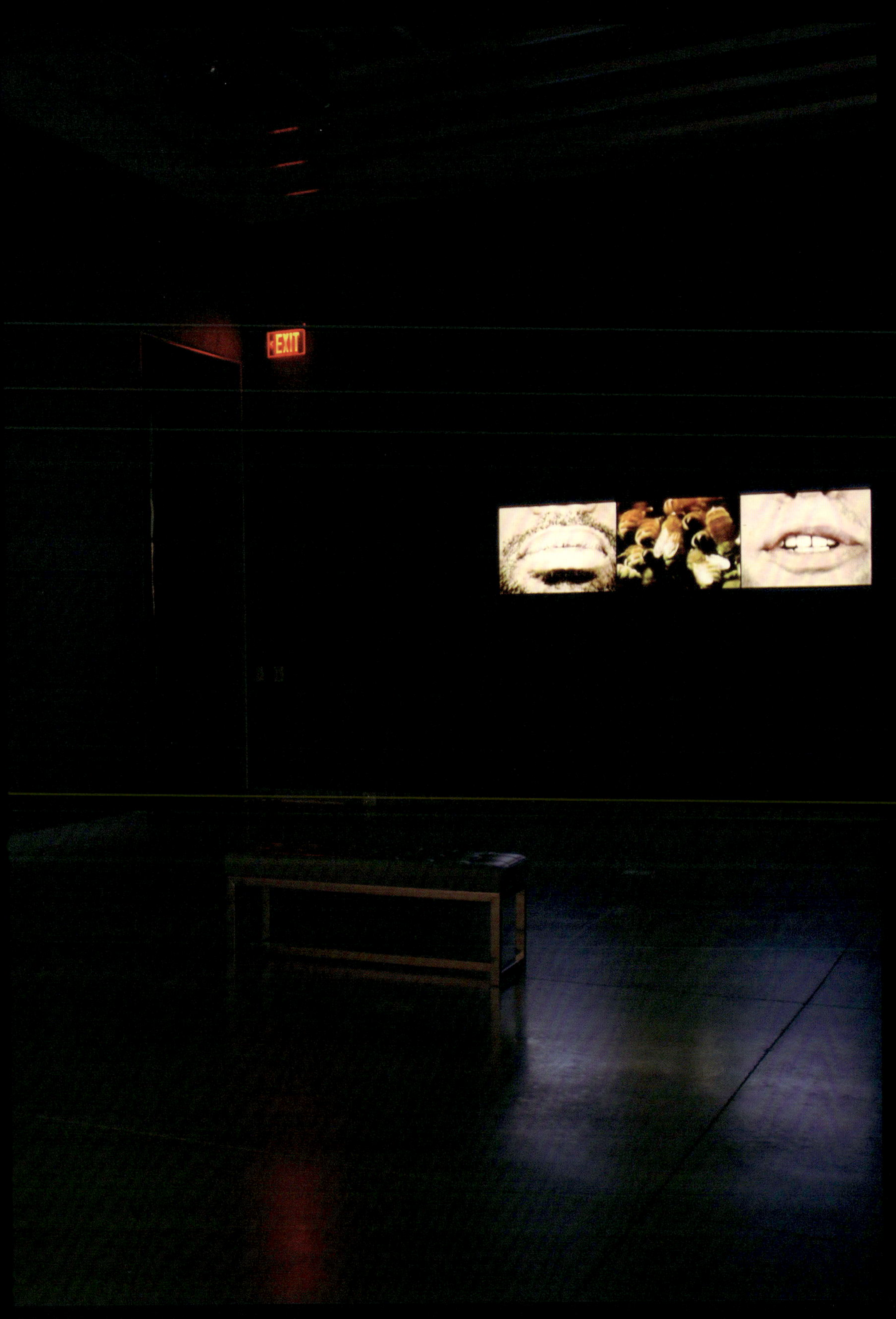

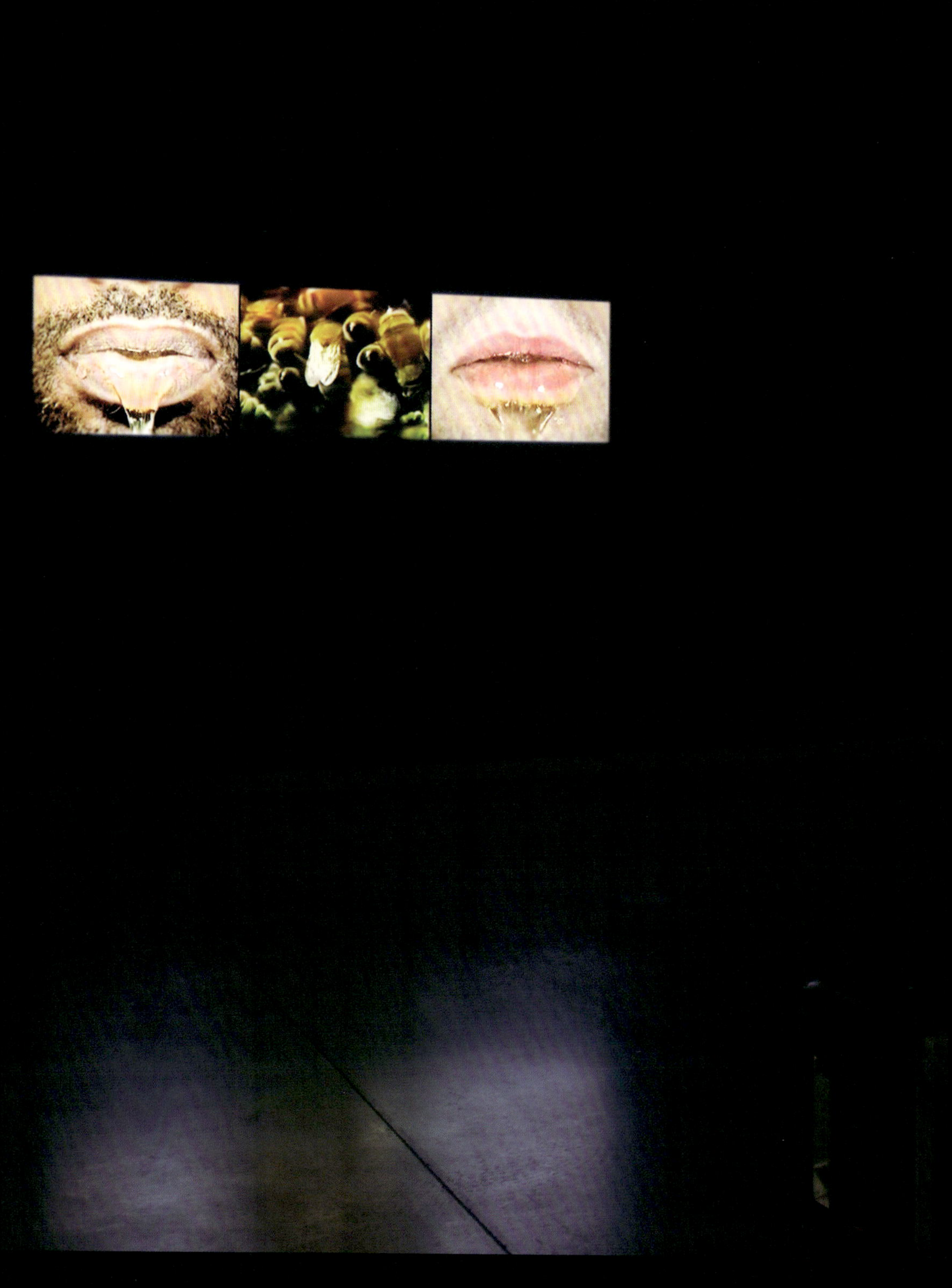

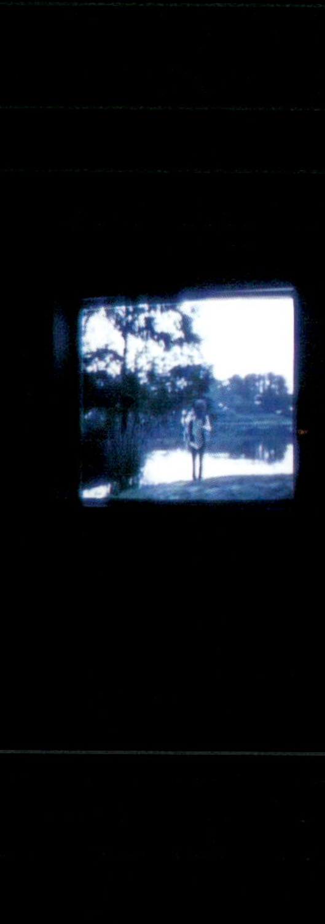

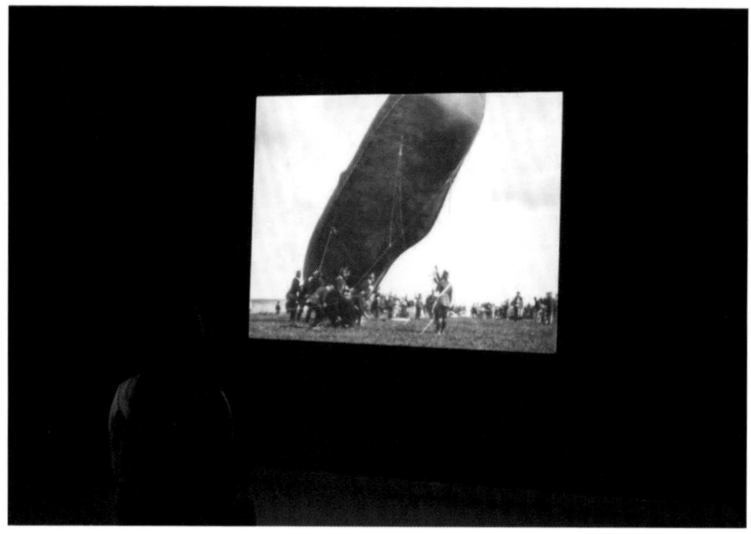

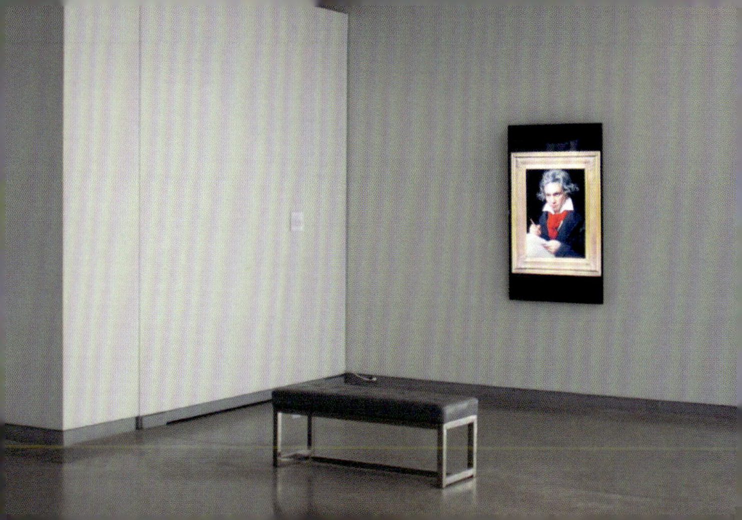

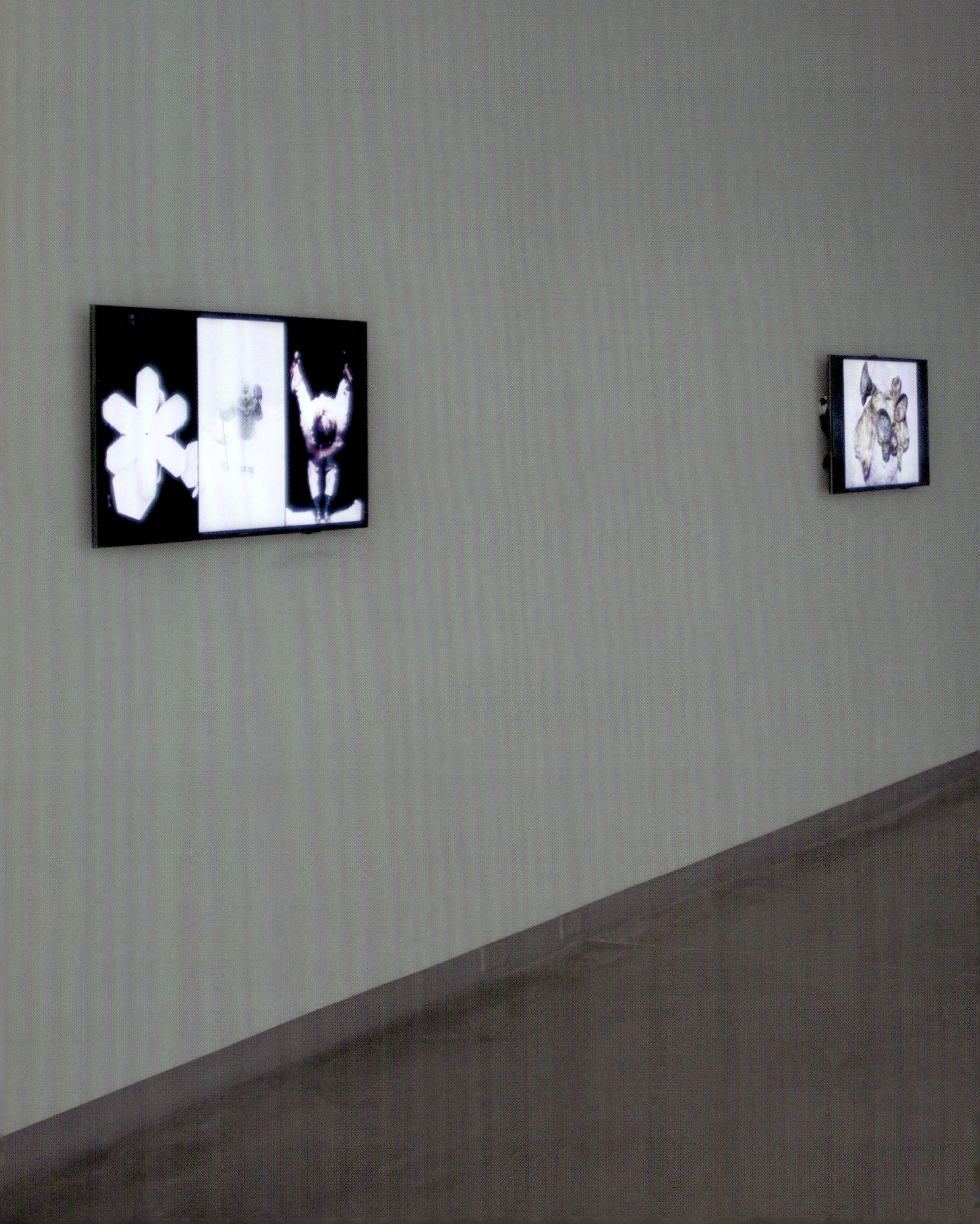

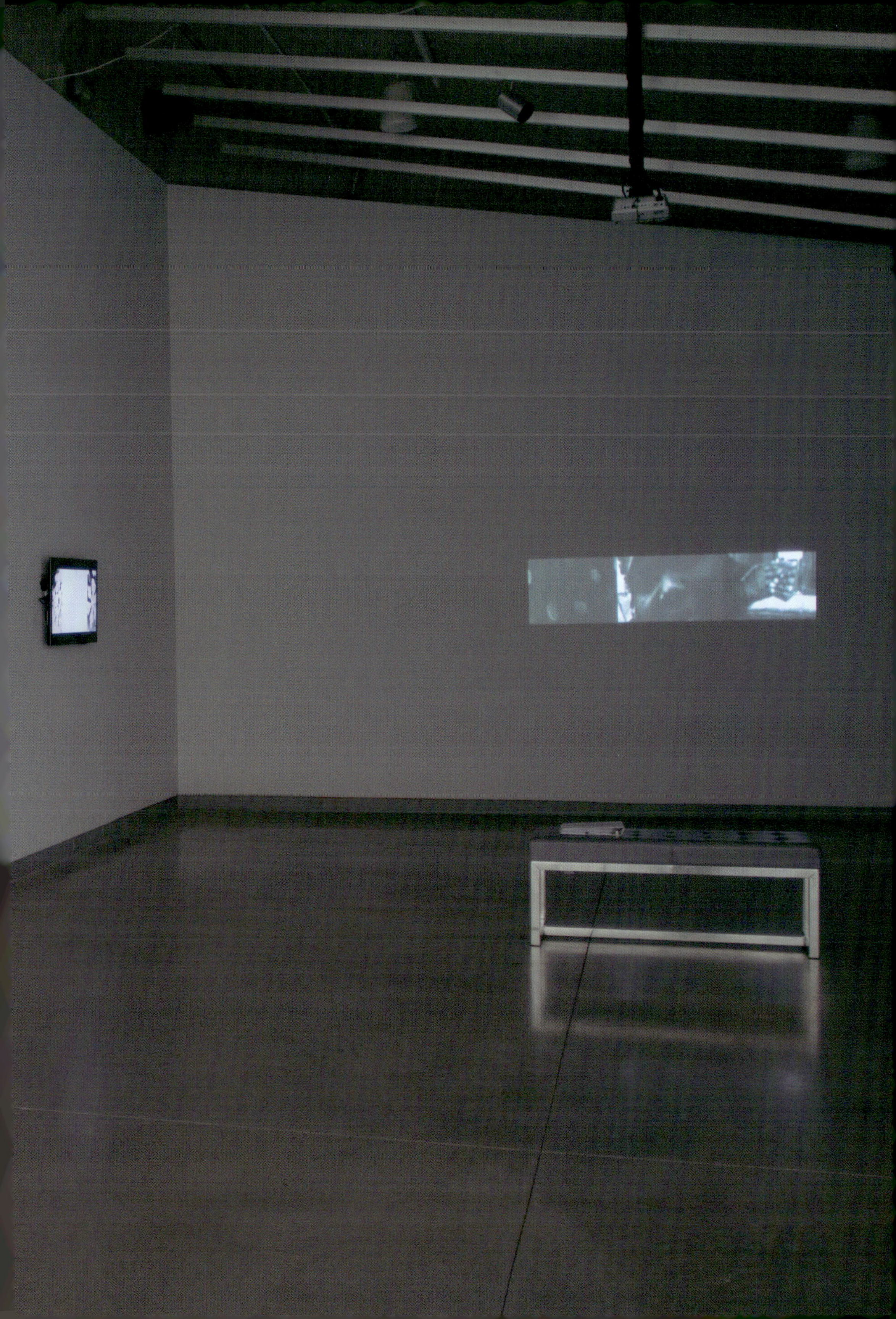

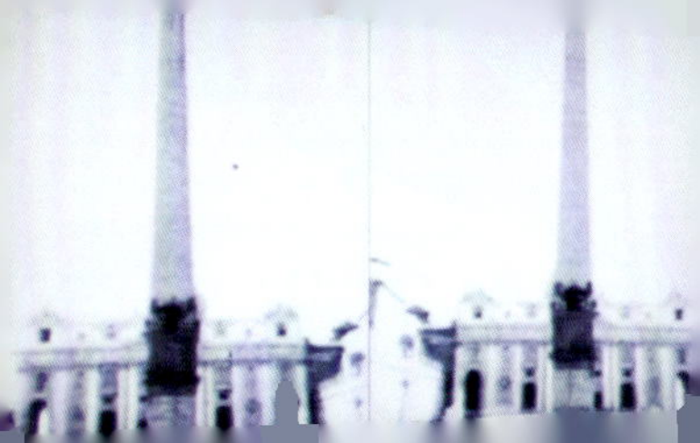

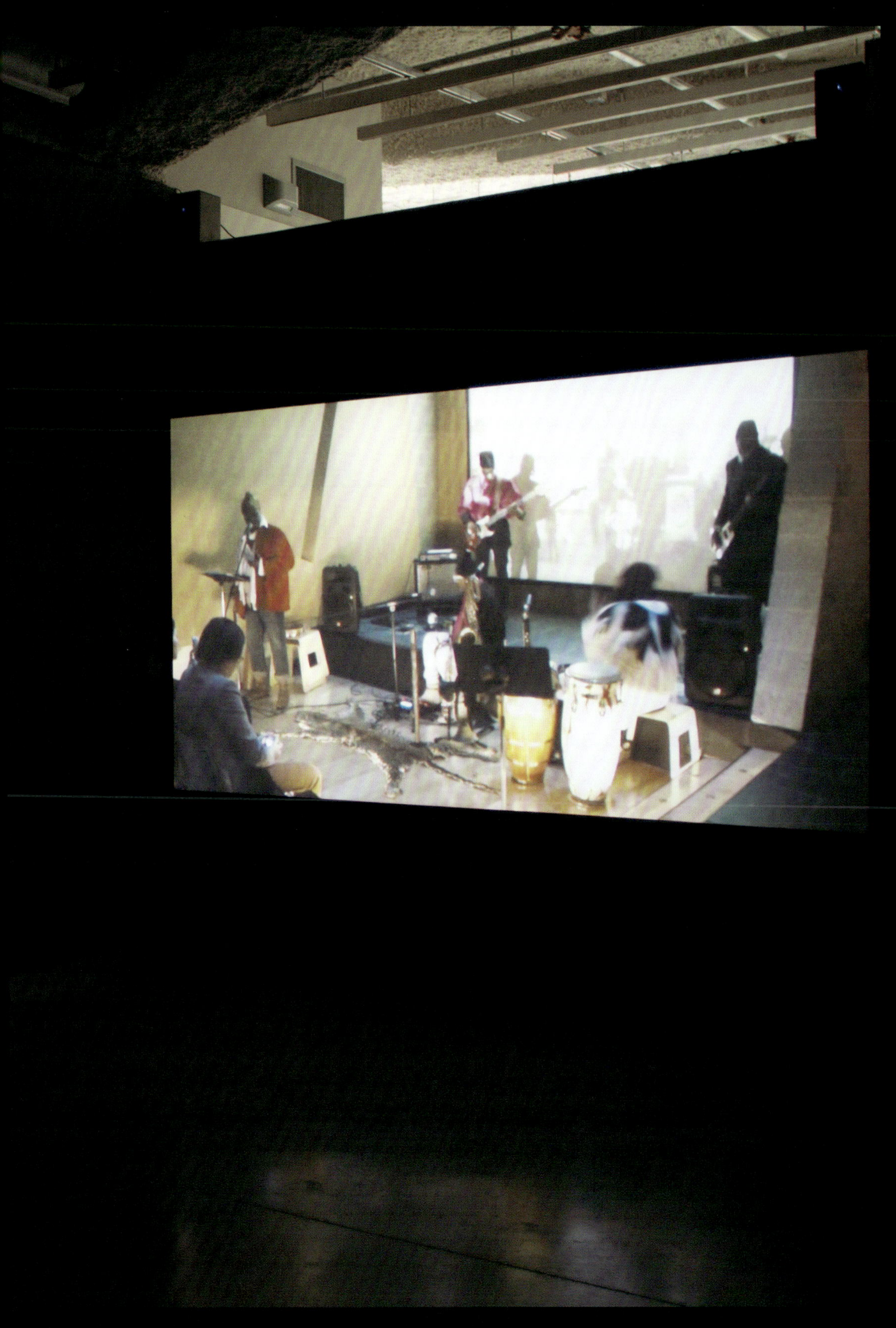

LORNA SIMPSON

In Conversation with Kendra Paitz

KP: You and Terry were friends for a long time. How did you first meet?

LS: We met many years ago on the Lower East Side, through art historian Kellie Jones. I was helping her move and she said, "Oh, I also called my friend Terry," and he showed up.

When was that?

It must have been sometime around 1987.

Terry performed in your 2004 film, *Cloudscape*. I was watching it again a few days ago and was struck by its profundity. Alone and whistling, Terry is slowly enveloped by fog before the video reverses and cycles through again. It's impossible to see it now without thinking about Terry's presence and absence. How did partnering for that project come about and what was it like to work with him?

I had the desire to make another project based on *Easy to Remember*, a piece I had created in 2001. The music for it was generated by humming as opposed to singing or speaking. I wanted to do another piece that involved musicality of the body, so I decided to focus on whistling. These works were structured on the premise of loops, and I wanted the structure of the loop to affect the melody.

Many of my early works, and even new works, include people that are in my life. It's a very natural way for me to work. I asked Terry to participate because I wanted him to not only perform the piece but also select the music. I cannot read music anymore; it was a childhood gift and I lost that ability. I had a songbook of spirituals from 1905—*Twenty-four Negro Melodies: Transcribed for the Piano* by composer S. Coleridge-Taylor. I asked Terry to choose a song with an interesting melody that was both familiar and unfamiliar, and to select a sequence to work with as a loop. As I look through that book now, the bookmark for the song that Terry selected is gone. So, at this moment, I am not sure which one it was. This 1905 collection of songs was both made possible and preserved by the efforts and talents of faculty and students and Jubilee Singers at Fisk, Hampton, and Tuskegee. At the time, I did not make the literal connection of this legacy to Terry's family history. I had chosen a songbook that was at the heart of Terry's early engagement with music, and his family's history of education. His uncle Rutherford was a physics teacher at Fisk University and later became the president of the university. Terry's father got his master's degree at Fisk; his younger brother attended Tuskegee University; and his sister went to Hampton University.

Cloudscape was shot at Sean Kelly Gallery in Chelsea, New York. Setting up the lighting, manipulating a fog machine, and asking Terry to do it all in one take

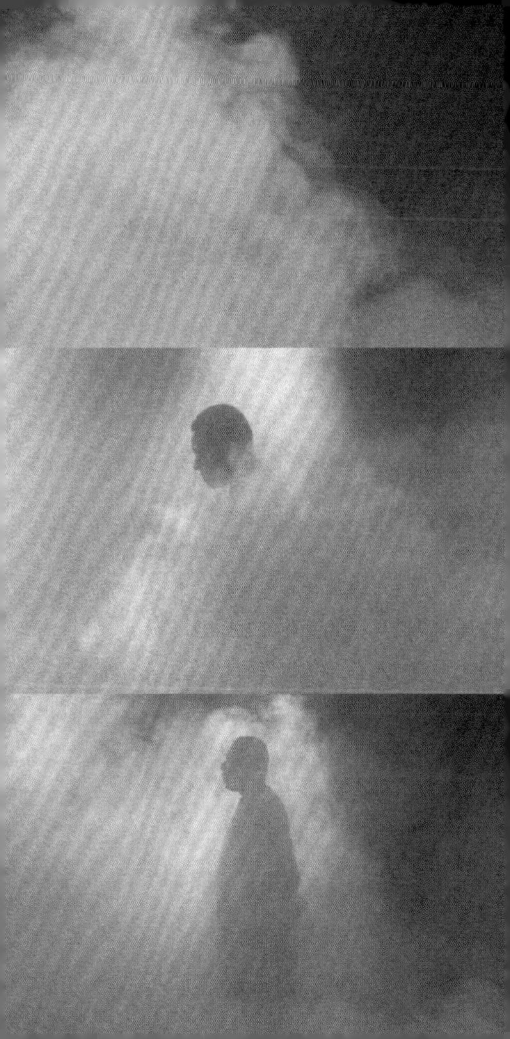

were important choices. It was shot on film the first time, which was lovely, but it was a nightmare in terms of technology because once transferred, the image had a lot of noise and was artifacting. It was digitally incoherent. I had to reshoot it a year later in exactly the same way but in high-definition video.

It's moving to learn about the songbook's connection to Terry's family history—so appropriate, given the deep emphasis he placed on connecting historical threads. And although challenging to make, the resulting video is seamless and speaks beautifully about impermanence.

I was aware of how ephemeral it was while I was making it. Of course, I didn't think about it in terms of Terry's longevity, but I definitely thought of presence and absence in terms of both the piece and the viewer, duration, and the shift to the sequence going in reverse. There are a lot of metaphors that one could draw upon with regard to mortality and memory. What I was aware of was that we kept it simple and gave it our full creative expression and we came up with a mesmerizing work.

Did you talk about collaborating on any projects?

No, we didn't. I have a deep appreciation for music that operates in many of my works. Our collaboration led to a collaboration much later with Jason Moran. Terry and I never spoke again about working together, but I never expected that there wouldn't be the possibility to do so at another point in the future.

Terry has been celebrated as an educator and mentor. Was it a struggle for him to find a balance between teaching and making work?

Actually, no. Terry loved teaching. As I mentioned, he came from a family with deep engagement in African American education; he loved being part of the academic environment and being a mentor. He had a very clear sense of how to balance that with his own

work, and he took the time he needed. For one of his last big projects, he embarked on a boat trip to the Arctic Circle, following Matthew Henson's path. Beautiful work came out of that trip. Both teaching and mentoring were really important to him, and I never got the impression that he would quit doing that to spend "more time" on his work. The dynamic of the back and forth—the exchange—was important to him. He made time for his work, and knew that he was valued as a professor who was actively making his own work.

The integrity of his practice is evident: from the unsung figures he studied, to the immersive research he conducted, to the abstract works he created.

He was a committed artist—to his own beliefs, to the kind of work he wanted to make, to how he wanted to make it. He also believed strongly in the intention behind his work. Terry—as an artist, musician, and intellectual—had an encyclopedic mind in terms of prose, poetry, music, and history.

He was masterful when it came to the possibilities and nuances of language. Although his work was conceptually rigorous, Terry often imparted a sense of magic or wonder. Do you think he was uniquely suited to do so? There are many artists who *try* to do that.

A lot of what Terry's work embraced—in bringing together a broad range of artistic disciplines—had to do with his commitment to live performance, improvisation, and collaboration. That is present in all of his work. The Lone Wolf Recital Corps is a perfect example. He was very aware of all those things all the time in all of his work. The magic comes from that sense of being present in the performance and the collaboration that takes place within that context. His imagination extended to the sculptural works, echoing the same beauty and intensity.

This exhibition focused on Terry's videos, so I included some documentation of his performances that incorporated videos, and, as a one-night event, I screened the "Facets" performance he did at the Tang Museum. It obviously wasn't the same as seeing it live…

But if you think of other artists—the relics of material from Ana Mendieta, for example—that archive of information becomes evidence of the work. It's different from the performance itself, but watching it and talking about it is valuable for understanding the scope of the artist's language.

I love that he brought so many people together, whether the shifting group that formed Lone Wolf or the students he would include when he was performing at universities. They were wonderful gestures of openness.

Right, that process was so important. Sharing one's work within an educational setting really opens up those students, or that institution, to different ways of working together and to depths of expression. What happens when you just let go and participate or give your attention to listen? Does it generate an idea for something else? By sharing his process, he opened up a more dynamic way of sharing ideas. That, to me, was his gift to academic environments. They really received the gift of observing his process to understand and question their own thinking and assumptions.

Terry increased awareness of revolutionary people like W. E. B. Du Bois, Matthew Henson, and John Brown. His research on Brown started because he was invited to realize a project in Akron, Ohio, where Brown had been a sheep farmer. And he developed his work addressing Lightnin' Hopkins for a project in Houston, where the legendary blues musician had lived. I don't think Terry always chose subjects based on exhibition locations though. Did he discuss how he made some of those decisions?

Terry appreciated, admired, and took inspiration from individuals who stood their moral ground at a time when their voice was neither popular nor respected, and even considered to be bold and dangerous. I believe that Terry's intellectual interests broadly spanned the geographical map of North America and the continent's full history.

In talking about his *Synapse (from Black Beethoven)* video, Terry said that he wanted to make work about Beethoven because he overcame hearing loss and touched generations of people with his music. He also wanted to acknowledge questions about Beethoven's Moorish ancestry but it seems that many people focus exclusively on that aspect.

When you think about the various ways that American and European identity is constructed, the canon of history likes to have things boxed in a very tight vacuum with intended omissions of the influences, contributions, and struggles of its evolving population. Accordingly, Beethoven's identity could only exist as a certain type of man. You mentioned Terry pushing back at boundaries or stances of power, and his investment in the complexity of identity is also a stance in his work. To portray Beethoven relative to North Africa was, in Terry's mind, part of the history and should not be excluded from the conversation about North America and Europe and their relationship to Africa.

I'm hoping that these conversations—telling portions of Terry's story through the words of people who knew him well—can be a step toward further highlighting his concerns. It seems that he had such an independent spirit. Who were some of the artists, or some of his peers, who influenced his practice?

Terry had a longtime friendship with David Hammons, and they both shared a passion for music. You can see an affinity in their work in the use of syntax, poetry, metaphor, language, music, found ordinary objects, the ephemeral, and the performative. I believe it was a very rich friendship for Terry to have had. How could it not have been? As we can all see, Hammons' work continues to expand, and from the very beginning,

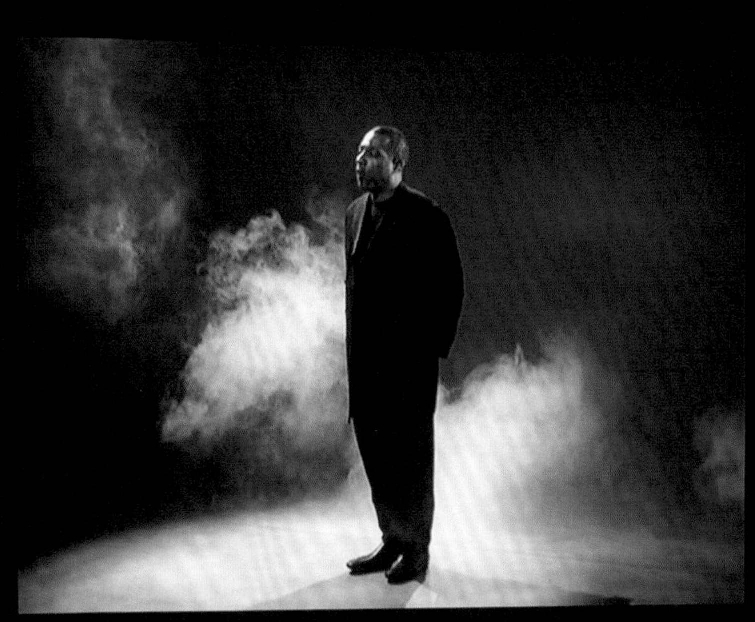

Installation view of Lorna
Simpson's *Cloudscape*,
2004. Video projection with
sound, 11:00 minutes (loop).
Courtesy of the artist and
Salon 94, New York.

his artistic language has reflected the times we live in. Hammons' work has always been captivating and inspiring.

Terry made such strong work throughout his career and influenced many artists, but he had only recently started to gain widespread critical recognition for it. Did he know that he was going to be featured in Venice?

He had just done an interview with Okwui [Enwezor] for Ian's [Berry] book, and they were in deep conversation. Everything wasn't signed and sealed but I believe Terry knew that Okwui was interested in including *Muffled Drums* (2003) and a series of related sculptures as a starting point of conversations about inclusion of works in *All the World's Futures*, the 56th *Venice Biennale*, in 2015.

In the months before Terry died, he was immersed in his work; he was really working on many projects. He was excited about bringing them to fulfillment. He was anticipating, and could see the trajectory of, where things were going and the opportunities that were coming.

Do you know if he was engaged in any unfinished projects? I think that he may have still been developing some of the Matthew Henson-related work and the *Aviarium* birdsong pieces.

Yes, *Aviarium*. The readymade elements were very elaborately constructed. He had assembled a few of them with the assistance of the staff from Salon 94, and had provided detailed drawings and specs on the assembly of each one. The layout drawings of each are really beautiful. He was literally putting the final touches on the ones that were exhibited in the 2014 *Whitney Biennial* at the time of his death.

I distinctly remember approaching and walking under those silent sculptural songs at the Whitney. Before we finish talking, I wonder if you have a favorite memory with Terry?

I was having dinner by myself at the bar of a restaurant in Brooklyn called Roman's. I was seated by myself on a barstool finishing a glass of wine and my dinner, and suddenly someone grabbed me from behind. It was in such a way that I couldn't move or turn around. He started whispering in my ear very sweetly, saying things like, "So, how you doing? Where have you been? What are you doing here by yourself?" I was thinking, "Who could this be?" His embrace was warm and all encompassing; it seemed like a boyfriend, but it couldn't be a boyfriend. I was very confused. I finally turned around and it was Terry. Merele was sitting nearby and they were both laughing hysterically because they could tell that I didn't know who it was or what was happening. But that was Terry's sense of humor, his warmth. He was very passionate, and also very loving and very kind. I guess I looked really pathetic sitting there by myself, hunched over eating at the bar after a long day of working in the studio. I moved to their table and joined them for dinner and we had a lovely time. He and Merele brightened my evening. I'll never forget that. I thought, "Who is this?" But, of course, it was Terry.

Several other people have talked about his warmth and generosity. What a wide-reaching impact he had. It's a significant point of pride that Terry was an alumnus of Illinois State University. At the exhibition's opening reception, we announced that our School of Art has endowed a memorial scholarship in his honor. So many people have worked together to make this happen.

It's a wonderful tribute and in the tradition of how he worked and shared his work. It's lovely that his mission and legacy continue.

———

Lorna Simpson is a Brooklyn-based artist who exhibits her work internationally. She was close friends with Terry Adkins.

JOSHUA MOSLEY

In Conversation with Kendra Paitz

KP: Did you know Terry before beginning your position at the University of Pennsylvania?

JM: No, we both began teaching at Penn in 2000.

How did you begin working together on some of his projects?

We started with sculptural projects. Terry had ideas for new pieces that could be worked out through computer modeling and then visualized for his proposals for public commissions. Only a few of those pieces were made though.

What was an example of one that wasn't made?

We had developed large, concave, mirrored, satellite dish-shaped sculptures as part of a proposal for a new park.

You worked closely with Terry to animate several of his videos. Can you talk a little bit about that process?

That began when Terry was thinking about his *Black Beethoven* project. We were talking about the Michael Jackson video, the one with the faces morphing continuously, and he was asking how to do that. We started to experiment with how we might morph a painting into a photograph.

After a conversation like that, Terry would usually send me images to run a test. It was a back-and-forth process to see how a piece could work. Many of the videos were created in two steps: one using his intuition and another for calibrating. For example, for some animations, he would give me thirty images and say that each should be on the screen for nine seconds. He determined things like the order and if the images should play backwards. One time, he sent me a graph mapping out all the edits. I would follow those instructions and send him the movie. After he saw the video, he usually made one change like, "Nine seconds is too fast. Make it eighteen." Then we'd be done. He would ask what I thought of the work and we would talk about it, usually conversing about how the pieces were functioning as video artworks. His videos were usually experimental at the beginning. Then he would develop very strong ideas about how he wanted to put them together and he'd come back to me to revise.

He kept reworking many of the "completed" versions over time?

We went back to several of the videos later, sometimes years later, to change the music or rework the images. Terry was always applying for grants or residencies. When he wanted to show the Beethoven video several years after making it, the piece really needed to be re-made in HD, so we made a new version. The first

NEW SERIES, AMERICAN VIEWS.
J. W. & J. S. MOULTON, SALEM, MASS.
Harper's Ferry, W. Va. Scenery.

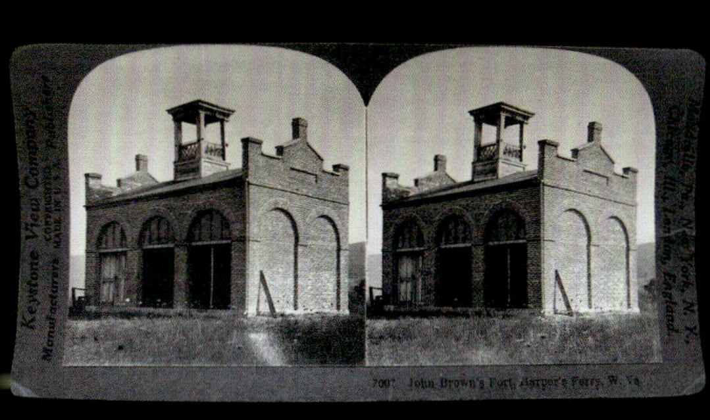

Keystone View Company
Manufacturers
COPYRIGHTED
MADE IN U.S.A.
Publishers
Meadville, Pa., New York, N. Y.,
Chicago, Ill., London, England.
7007   John Brown's Fort, Harper's Ferry, W. Va.

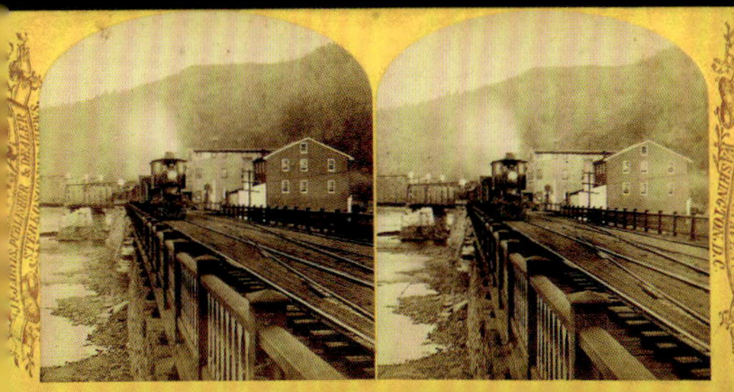

J. W. & J. S. MOULTON, PUBLISHER & DEALER, STEREOSCOPES.
135 PENNSYLVANIA AVENUE, WASHINGTON, D.C.

version was made for a 2004 show in Philadelphia. Then in 2007, Terry reworked the music and found a higher-resolution image of the painting. When he showed the video at the Tang, he wanted it to be on a vertical screen. At that point, he had to start figuring out how to present his video work because he was being included in a large number of shows and his work began to be collected.

You introduced Terry to Ken Jacobs' *Capitalism: Slavery,* a video that activates a stereograph image of people picking cotton. Terry used stereograph cards in several of his video works, including *Behold Harpers Ferry, Miy Paluk 1866,* and *Flumen Orationis.* The flickering between the left and right side of the cards introduces such motion into the exhibition space and invites the viewer into these historical images in an unexpected way. Did Terry talk about any other reasons why he was drawn to using the cards?

He was trying to find a way to work with the stereo cards he had been collecting and I remembered Ken Jacobs' film. After we looked at that, and Scott Stark's animated stereo photographs of Angel Beach, we experimented with Terry's collection of stereographic cards relating to John Brown in a similar way. We animated between the left and right photograph and nudged the alignment until the images cracked open and became three-dimensional. At the time, I was teaching a landscape architecture class at Harvard and was working with a similar idea of layering space in landscape. I started thinking about that for a piece I did when I was in Rome in 2006.

Was he buying the cards online or discovering them during his travels?

I think he was buying some of them on eBay, but he was always shopping so his collection probably came from many sources. The subject matter of his cards seemed to be vast, but, in retrospect, when the works came together, his collection seemed very specific.

Maybe there was something about the cards being an index that interested him. For instance, it's kind of amazing that he transformed a collection about early balloon flight into a piece about Jimi Hendrix as a paratrooper. I think he saw the cards operating similarly to an image resource folder—of another time and place—in the public library. We were both excited that the images were stereo because we could unlock them in a slightly different and deeper way. When they begin to flicker, you instantly sense there is much more information. What's the John Brown/railroad one?

Behold Harpers Ferry.

Yeah, yeah. I really remember unlocking those images by flipping left and right. Being able to position your eye, or position yourself in a field or in relation to the railroad tracks, was exciting to both of us. Having a historical image and then being able to re-spatialize it in that moment was incredible.

I projected that video at a fairly large scale in a darkened gallery and the train engine looked like it was coming into the room. And the comet seems to be hurtling through space. I saw several stereo cards featuring astronomical phenomena on his hard drive but, as far as I know, he only used that single image. Do you know why he picked that particular one to resonate with Brown's story?

I think he had more than twenty comet images to work with and he wanted to use one as a break between the John Brown images instead of inserting a black screen. He said he wanted "the feeling of cosmic destiny to be there." He found connections in the most disparate things that then made sense when he assembled them. Shortly after Terry arrived at the American Academy in Rome, he told me that he had found a connection between Charles Follen McKim (one of the architects of the Academy building) and John Brown. McKim's father had helped John Brown's wife following Brown's execution. Terry had several ideas about what to work on in Rome, but that discovery moved him to revisit Harpers Ferry and John Brown.

One of the aspects of Terry's work that I respect so much is the deep research that he engaged in. For his Matthew Henson-related pieces, he actually went to the North Pole, as well as to Alaska. You mentioned that he had access to a special camera at the Anchorage Museum. He used that to record his jumping for *Miy Paluk 1866*?

He was in Alaska for a residency to prepare for an exhibition and he had access to the museum. They had a science exhibit in which visitors could see themselves in slow-motion playback. After hours, Terry set up his camera and shot footage of himself from the exhibit's screen. I think he did that for several nights while experimenting with different clothing and actions. At the North Pole, he used a Canon camera and a GoPro to make videos of himself standing in the snow and wearing different coats. The *Miy Paluk* video was finalized on April 16, 2012, a week before his show at the Palais de Tokyo in Paris.

In addition to the footage of him both jumping and standing motionless, he also incorporated stereo images of microscopic snowflakes in *Miy Paluk 1866*. Were those from a collection at the museum?

That's funny, I remember seeing those images online first. I think we did something with them before he went to Rome, and then we did more when he was there. We were initially using images that he found online—probably on a scientist's website—but he had better scans of them later. In one of the videos, he used footage of an actual snowfall, which I think he shot from his studio balcony in Rome.

We exhibited that one, *Dante Paradiso XXVII*. The falling snow is bordered by stereo images of snowflakes, as in *Miy Paluk*. The layers of sound in that one are so incredible—with music, what sounds like a crackling fire, and Terry's and a woman's voices reading Dante's passages in English and Italian, respectively. That crackling sound makes the snowflakes more mysterious too; at times, they look like ashes.

Going back to your question about the comet, Terry only started talking about those astronomical images when he was in Rome. I don't want to speculate too much but it's hard not to. The American Academy is on a hill and behind it is Casa Rustica, a bar that used to be a farmhouse. I think it's where Galileo first tested the telescope. I told Terry about it when I was in residence at the Academy in 2006. I think there must have been something about that site that related to the comet image too, but he had made work relating to both astronomy and Dante prior to that.

In one of our earlier conversations, you mentioned that Terry liked the timing of many of his works to be divisible by nine or twelve in relation to Beethoven's symphonies. The influence of music on his practice is evident in many ways. With the double- and triple-channel videos, in particular, there's so much happening with the cadences, the ways that the images and sounds come in and out. Some of them are also punctuated by blank spaces and silence. Did he talk about other things he was interested in with the timing?

Not a whole lot. Eighteen would be the other number but it seemed to me that that had something to do with the nine, in terms of things going backward and forward. In the case of the soundtrack for *Synapse (from Black Beethoven)*, there was an idea of two things crossing in opposite directions. The sound is going in two directions at the same time.

Terry was always excited about his harmonizer, a sound processing unit similar to what Laurie Anderson used. It was an early electronic, after-the-analog thing called the Eventide Harmonizer. I guess that played a non-numerical role in his compositional structuring. It's great you're doing this show because some of Terry's decisions that might have evolved from his music became visual in his structuring of videos.

Terry was such a performer. Did he improvise a lot with the sound for his videos?

I don't know how much he improvised but I never saw him write anything he was playing. He was often making the music for the pieces very specifically. For the ones that we worked on, he would come up with something for the soundtrack and then edit it on the computer in the following weeks. He used an old upright bass for the sound for *Black Beethoven*. I remember that piece at an earlier stage. It became more layered but I'm not sure if that was because he was adding recordings to it or because he was working with different kinds of processors and ways of layering to get the kind of resonances that he wanted.

He would always find a way to work with the sound so there was a parallel between it and what was happening with the images. I think he would watch the movies late at night and play around with the sound, but not in a precise, locked-in way. He would have his laptop open to watch while working on sound on another computer. He wasn't the kind of person who would make small changes; it was always in broad, decisive strokes.

It's been so powerful to sit in the gallery dedicated to Flumen Orationis. It's incredible to listen to the entirety of Martin Luther King Jr.'s "Why I Am Opposed to the War in Vietnam" speech, especially set to Jimi Hendrix's "Machine Gun," but it's also crushing to realize that, five decades later, so many people still need to heed his words.

You know, when I was talking about the soundtrack before—a better way to put that would be a "crossing resonance," where one thing is going forward and one thing is going in reverse. There's a beautiful crossing resonance in that King and Hendrix piece. When Terry mixed the sound forward and backward, the layering created a harmonic third thing.

You are an artist who makes animations, among other things. What stands out to you about Terry's videos? Or his practice in general?

It's interesting how he was able to sustain a focus on abstract images as a way to connect with the historical research he was doing. Whether or not it was a spiritual way of working, he was looking for something in the air around the person that would surpass the factual points of their lifetimes. He was always after something deeper.

I've been talking with several people about Terry's influence on his students and his continued mentorship of them after graduation. What was his presence on campus and in the classroom like? I imagine there was a significant void after his passing.

For 13 years, we were good colleagues; we were really working together on building a department. There's so much I could say! He would find a way to bond with the students who needed it most. He supported them in terms of their confidence and helped them to believe in parts of their spirit that they hadn't felt confident about before. He was always on the lookout for a student who was about to emerge; he called each of those students "the mouse that roared." He described our program that way too.

He would bond with graduate students in many ways. He would have this dialogue that could be anywhere and at any time of day. There would be a continuous conversation about life and work. It would start when the person had just applied to graduate school and would continue forever. And those students would often be involved in different aspects of the production of Terry's work—maybe physically dragging objects across campus, traveling with him, or driving him. He would drop in at their studios to give them a critique or advice when they were least expecting him.

He also taught the graduate sculpture seminar and he would usually pick two readings from books that were outside the canon of what art schools typically tell you to read. The topic of one would often result in an exhibition of work the students made in response to the text. Terry picked texts he felt were open enough for the students to discover ideas that would help them both find themselves and generate work. That was usually true; many of the students responded strongly to the readings.

What were some examples of those texts?

Mirror of the Intellect by Titus Burckhardt, *Things Fall Apart* by Chinua Achebe, and *Moby Dick*.

It's nice to know more about how Terry operated as a professor. Do you have a favorite memory with him?

We were hanging out one night and I told him I wanted to buy a Muybridge print that was being auctioned on eBay. The photo sequence of a walking mastiff was taken at Penn when Muybridge was working on his large series of motion studies. The only problem was that the auction ended in the middle of my seminar class. Terry said, "That's simple; just call a break when the auction is ending and bid." I told him that the auction ended only thirty minutes into my class, and he said, "So call an early break." The next day, my class took a very early break. The auction quickly turned into a bidding war with the price going up 400% in the last two minutes. I lost. As I was walking out of my office the phone rang and Terry—who was extremely excited—told me that he won the dog for me. I start laughing, and yelled, "Terry, that was me!"

—

Joshua Mosley and Terry Adkins were colleagues at the University of Pennsylvania. A Philadelphia-based artist, Mosley is Professor and Chair of the Department of Fine Arts in the School of Design at University of Pennsylvania.

DEMETRIUS OLIVER

In Conversation with Kendra Paitz

KP: You were Terry's student at the University of Pennsylvania. Did you choose that MFA program specifically to study with him or did you find your way into his classes once you were there?

DO: I wasn't aware of Terry before I applied, but once accepted into the program, I started researching him and knew right away that he was someone I would want to study with. A *Sculpture Magazine* interview with Terry was included in the materials for new students. Everything he was talking about really resonated with me. He was fond of telling people that I took his sculpture seminar for four semesters when only two semesters were required.

What was Terry like as a professor? I know how much he valued education and would imagine that his courses were rigorous and his expectations were high.

In his seminar class, he always pushed students to work outside of their chosen mediums. He pushed us to try something new, which, for some, opened up new possibilities. If you were a painter, you could make a sculpture. If you were a sculptor, you might try a performance in his class. All of his effort went toward ensuring that his students would not become generic artists upon graduation. His assignments were designed to make us respond to a particular text, film, or poem. Having that source provided parameters for our decision-making and provided the work with substance.

It seems like he embraced all the possibilities with his own work, in terms of his experimentation with mediums and processes. It's not surprising that he would bring that into the classroom. He was an educator for so many years. How did the students respond to him? Did he develop close relationships with many of them?

Teaching for Terry was as natural as breathing. He did it without much effort. He took a special interest in developing relationships with students in school and after graduation. He became a mentor to a number of us, even to artists who were not officially his students. He was fond of incorporating his students into his performances, or having them help with the preparations for a show. That dynamic is quite rare and the experience it provided was so valuable. Students got to witness the decision-making involved in an exhibition, as well as the rigorous nature of the demands he put on himself in the process.

We talked regularly. That's one of the things I miss the most about him. He wouldn't allow more than three weeks to go by without checking in. Anytime we talked, it was also about politics or current affairs; it wasn't just about art.

He became your mentor and the two of you continued a friendship after you graduated. With your interest in the celestial and your marriage of innovative materials

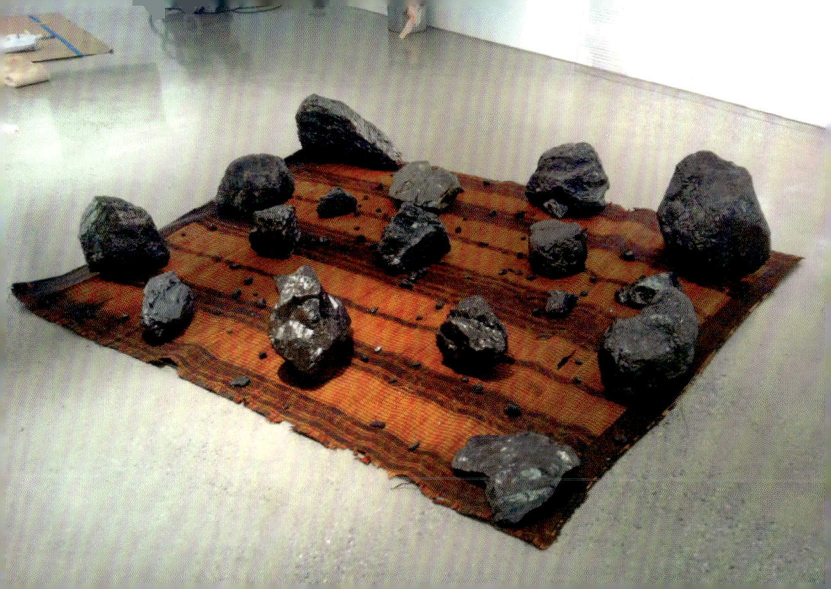

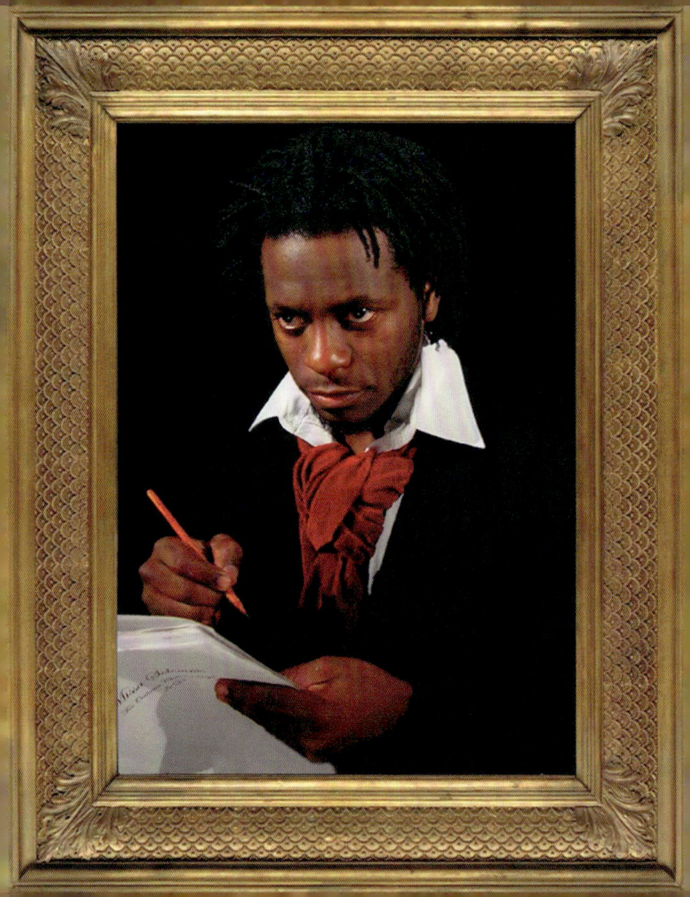

use and strong conceptual underpinnings, it seems that you and Terry must have been a good match for supporting and challenging one another.

Because we were both invested in materials and their potential for metaphor, it was always fun to collaborate. I felt like I got more out of the experience because I always gained a new perspective from his insight. Right before a solo show, I would often call him up, after sending him a jpeg, to ask for his feedback on a particular piece.

That's wonderful.

Yeah, he did that with quite a few of us who were close to him. It was actually pretty terrifying though. Jamal Cyrus and I would send him an image right before we did an exhibition and he would give us his honest opinion, which, many times we didn't want to hear right before an opening. So, it was beneficial but intimidating at the same time.

I feel like that sometimes when I finish my first solid draft of an essay and then give it to someone to look at. There are some analogies between the process of writing and making artwork. Our director has been writing and editing for years and it's such a luxury to have someone who will give honest critical feedback.

Mm hmm. That part I miss.

You took the photograph that Beethoven's image slowly transitions into for Terry's *Synapse (from Black Beethoven)* video.

I did. It's of Ernel Martinez, who was also one of Terry's students.

Did you talk to Terry about his other videos? For instance, I'm curious why he continued to use stereo cards in several of the videos after 2009.

I think it was the physicality. He was working with film but he was looking for ways to make it more material-like. By using two similar images and giving them a flickering, it almost provided a three-dimensional presence to the subject seen in the image. That's what I would assume about his inclination toward that way of making.

In *Behold Harpers Ferry*, he used an image of a comet, and because of the back-and-forth, that flickering, it looks like the comet is really moving.

I'd like to look at that.

Have you seen any of his more recent videos like *Miy Paluk 1866*? That's the one that features him jumping up and down in slow motion.

Yes, he was using some kind of machine or device that produced a low-resolution video. He was just doing it for fun; it wasn't even serious. But then he showed it to Okwui Enwezor, and Okwui just fell in love with the low-tech-ness of it. So it wasn't something he originally did to show. I don't know how much importance he gave to it at the time. It's a really beautiful video though.

I saw Blanche Bruce listed as a collaborator on your 2008 work, *Motus Librationis*. That title called to mind Terry's 2012 video *Flumen Orationis*. Did Terry embody Blanche Bruce for that work?

Blanche Bruce was a two-person collaborative we created in 2007 to hide Terry's authorship in the work we were collaborating on. Much later, he expanded it into a revolving membership, similar to the Sacred Order of the Twilight Brothers and Lone Wolf Recital Corps. He valued collaborations and always sought ways to incorporate others into his recitals, and he made no distinction between students and professionals. He was more interested in the "we" than the "me" aspect of making and sought ways to bring people from outside the art world into his work.

We often read about the influence of authors, musicians, and historical figures—Dante, Coltrane, W. E. B. Du Bois, among many others—on Terry's work. Who were some other figures, maybe even fellow contemporary artists, that he was interested in?

He preferred art of the anonymous tradition, as expressed in Chartres Cathedral, for example, or artifacts created by various cultures that served a purpose besides simple aesthetics in a given society.

You took part in the tribute to Terry at the Guggenheim Museum.

That was organized by Carrie Mae Weems, as you know. She wanted to suggest aspects of his performative style and the importance he placed on speech in his work. Ernel Martinez and I were opposite one another in the balcony of the Guggenheim's auditorium. We each spoke about recent projects and our debt to Terry as images of our respective work were projected on the screen.

I've been thinking about how the narrative of Terry's legacy is still emerging, and with his inclusion in major group exhibitions like the *Venice Biennale*, *Whitney Biennial*, and *Radical Presence*, among others, as well as the upcoming publication of the Tang Museum's 30-year retrospective catalogue, awareness about his work will only continue to grow. I realize that this must be emotional to discuss, but could you talk about Terry's artistic impact—for you and for others?

He saw his legacy continuing through his students. The principles and values that his students display are a reflection of his teaching and who he was as a person. I know this was important to him because of the number of younger artists he actively sought to mentor. With regards to the impact of his art, he demonstrated that abstraction could be infused with narrative to challenge people's understanding of biography.

Because his work has received so much critical attention in the past few years, is there anything you would like people to know about him that they may not already?

Terry was critical of a lot of image-based work that solely addressed identity and saw his work as a challenge to that predicament.

I've read a few interviews in which he was fairly vocal about that position. Could you talk a little bit more about that, not necessarily citing artists that he was critical of, but some of the things that he didn't respond to in that type of work?

Some of his work seems like it deals with identity but it really doesn't. He was looking at humanity and what it means to be human, but using different historical figures to express that—individuals he felt a kinship with in regard to shared values. His dedication to abstraction definitely set him apart, but also caused his career to suffer as figurative work by artists his age and younger demanded more market and curatorial attention. He had absolutely no interest in the current trend of deconstructing or examining identity. It's important to have that stance expressed and to understand what he was fighting for.

Do you have a favorite memory with Terry?

The contentment he displayed to me while at dinner in Philly a week before his passing. After being ignored and passed over for much of his career, he was finally starting to receive the recognition that he so desperately wanted and rightfully deserved.

Was the dinner for a particular occasion?

I was putting together my solo show at the Print Center. Anytime I was in Philly, I would try to visit him, so we went to his favorite restaurant near Penn's campus. He was actually scheduled to do a performance at the

Franklin Institute's planetarium in conjunction with
my exhibition, but he passed away a month before
that could occur. For the event I was going to project
some images on the ceiling as he performed. Over the
years, we've had a lot of discussions and some of them
voiced frustration about his lack of recognition and
the celebration of mediocrity he saw happening in the
art world at large. That dinner was the first time that
I saw him really at peace. He was selected to participate
in the *Whitney Biennial* that year and the Tate had
recently bought his *Muffled Drums* sculpture. He was
actually selling. For years he didn't have that, so he
was really happy about it.

—

*Demetrius Oliver was Terry Adkins' student at the University
of Pennsylvania from 2002–2004. He is an artist living in
New York City and teaching at Princeton University.*

VALERIE CASSEL OLIVER

In Conversation with Kendra Paitz

KP: How did you and Terry first meet? Did you know him before curating his work into your 2005 CAM Houston exhibition, *Double Consciousness: Black Conceptual Art Since 1970*?

VCO: I did not know him but I knew of him. I knew that the Blanton Museum at the University of Texas at Austin owned one of his works. Annette Carlozzi at the Blanton knew him and spoke highly of him. *Double Consciousness* was the first time I actually had any interaction with Terry. You know, he had a propensity to engage people in a "trial by fire" framework, so we had our trial in 2005. When I proposed to present *Sermonesque* and *Muffled Drums* in the exhibition, Terry never mentioned that the works needed to be activated. When he told me a week before the opening, I said, "Well, I wish we had unraveled that bit of the riddle sooner." Needless to say, we could not activate the works for the exhibition. Terry even threatened to pull them from the exhibition. It got really contentious at one point, but I simply implored him to keep them in. I just said, "The works are so integral to the concept of the exhibition, especially with your reference to Du Bois." I also said, "One day we'll have an opportunity to meet in person and I will look forward to that moment when I can look at you in your face and tell you exactly what I think about you."

A couple of years passed and then I had an opportunity to look him in the face. He was speaking at NYU as part of a conference that Deb Willis, Skip Gates, Thelma Golden, and a few other visionaries had the great fortune to create. Terry was speaking on a panel and he was very thoughtful in his comments. Afterwards, I stood with the many people who had come to thank him. When he turned to me, I said, "Hello, Terry, this is Valerie. Do you remember I told you we were going to meet? Well, today is the day." His eyes, I'll never forget, were massive as though he was thinking, "Oh my God, what did I say to this woman? What did I do?" I could tell that he was rifling through his database. I realized at that moment that he was just who he was, which deeply endeared him to me. I was a big fan of his work, but as a person, he was so contentious in my mind until I actually met him. I understood so much from that interaction. His passion and love, his insistence on making things right to honor people and places in history—those things were part of the fiber of who he was as a person. And I got it. It wasn't rocket science once I met him. I got who he was and it made me admire and respect him all the more for it.

Did you ever think of organizing a solo project or a retrospective of his work?

I was so thankful to hear that Ian [Berry] did the retrospective. I told Terry, "I love you. I love your work. I believe so much in who you are and what you do and why you do it. But life is short and I can't. I've got a kid.

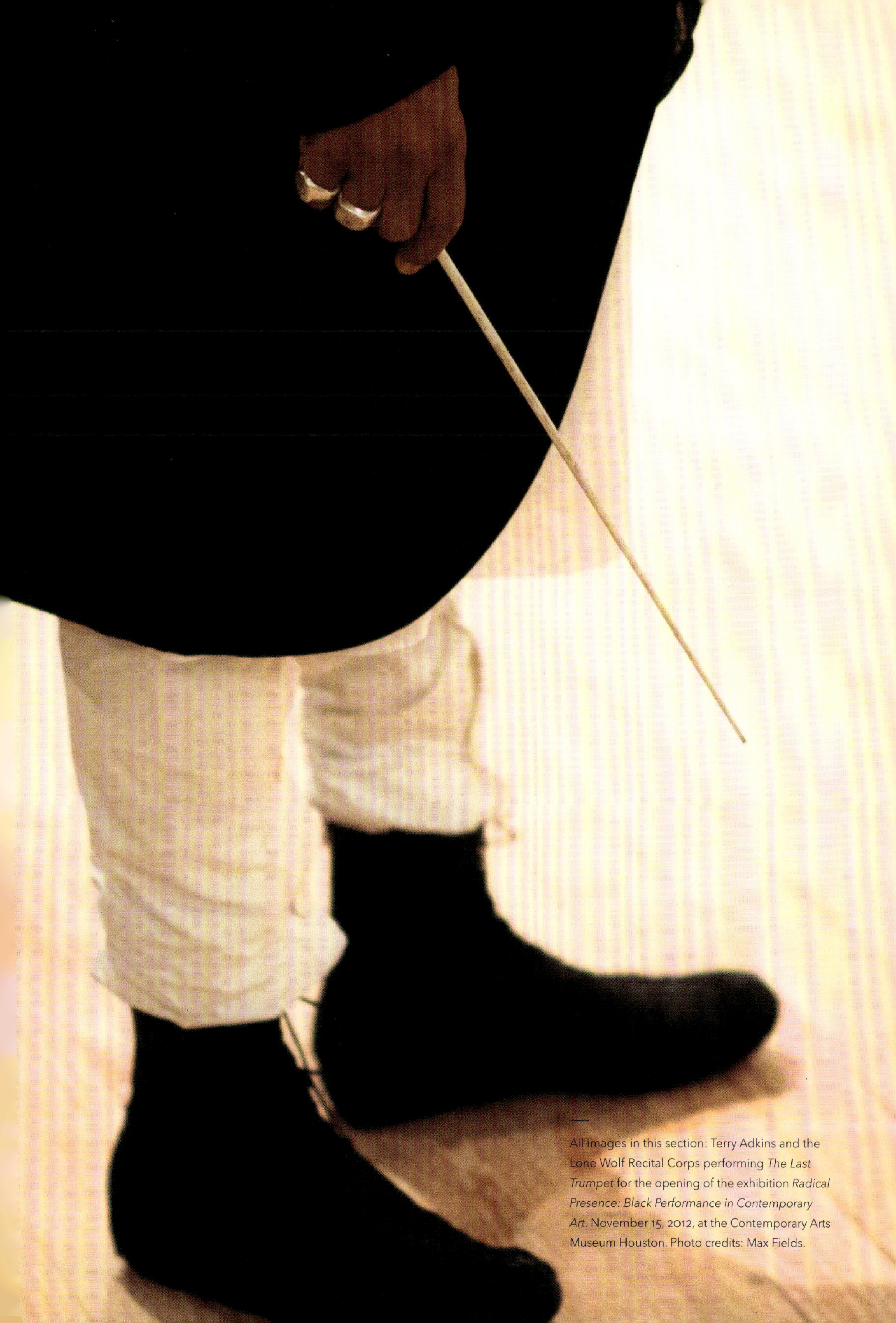

All images in this section: Terry Adkins and the Lone Wolf Recital Corps performing *The Last Trumpet* for the opening of the exhibition *Radical Presence: Black Performance in Contemporary Art*. November 15, 2012, at the Contemporary Arts Museum Houston. Photo credits: Max Fields.

I would end up doing something very dastardly to you." He could challenge you and that could be very off-putting, but everything was done out of love. He was always pushing, always challenging…not only you, but also himself, to always be better. You felt that instinctively. And he pushed all the artists that he taught and/or mentored, and they loved him for it! He would constantly challenge everyone to get to the next level. That's just the kind of person he was.

Although I met Terry in the year before he passed, we never had the opportunity to conduct a studio visit. Did you have several visits with him over the years? I assume they were different after that initial correspondence and later interaction.

Yes, definitely! He came to Houston in 2009 after proposing to do an Artist Round at Project Row Houses to celebrate Lightnin' Hopkins. For the project, he invited Sherman Fleming, Andrew Brown, and Charles Gaines, as well as George Smith, a sculptor

who is based in Houston. I had the chance to sit with them to discuss their work and to speak at length with Terry because I was planning to review the show. And that, honestly, was one of the turning points for the development of *Radical Presence*. Through those conversations, as well as those that I was having with Clifford Owens, I was able to begin compiling a history of black artists working in performance. It was during that time that I started talking with Terry and Sherman much more extensively about that history. They helped to shape that conversation for a different generation.

I was looking at the *Radical Presence* catalogue again this morning and noticed that you mentioned Terry as one of your many "teachers" regarding performance art.

It was very real. It was so helpful to listen to him talk about when performance entered into his work and why it became crucial. He also talked about when and where performance began to emerge among his peers.

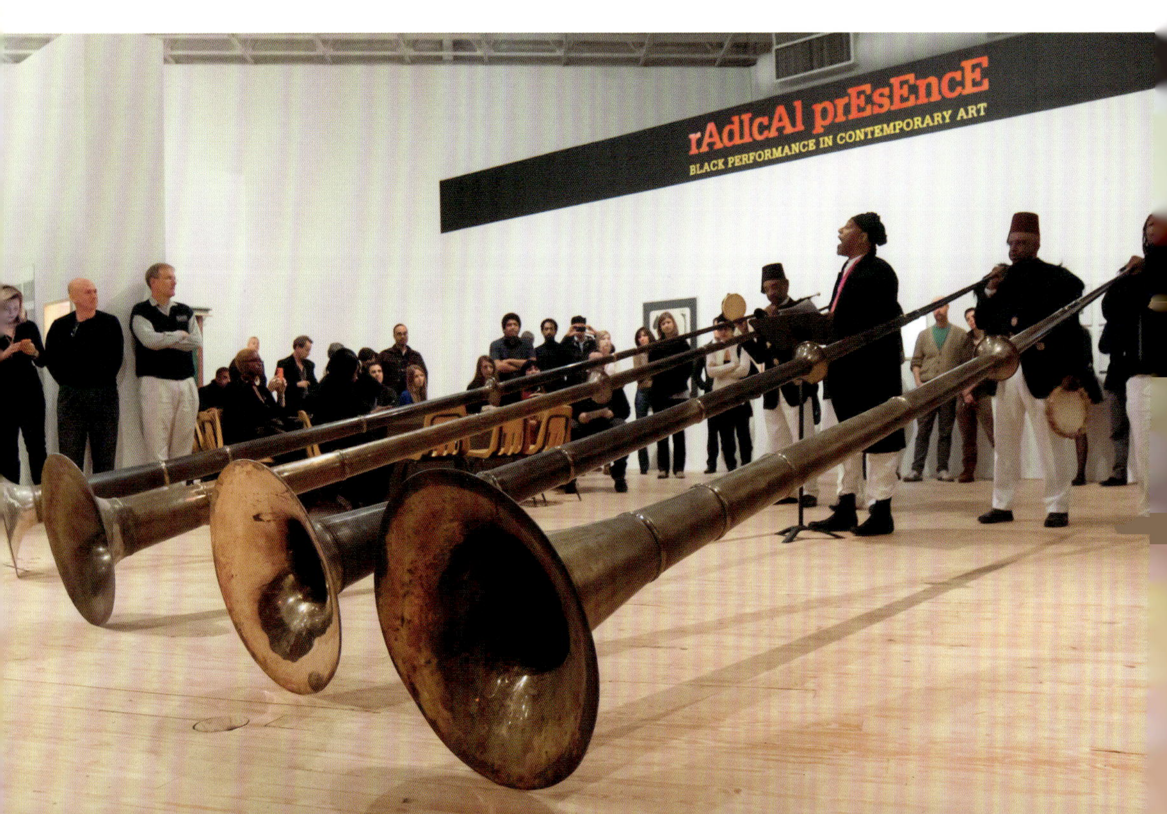

It was very important for me to get that part of the story. It helped me filter out a notion of what performance was, particularly coming out of the visual arts, and why it felt so necessary to be there alongside the visual object. It was the difference between trying to make the case for visual artists doing performance or just creating a different dimension of performance work that already existed, like theater, music, or dance. This is something completely different. Those conversations were invaluable to me.

Terry performed *The Last Trumpet* for the CAM Houston presentation of *Radical Presence*. Did he develop new collaborative relationships in your city?

He performed with musicians that were local. Jamal Cyrus, his former student and an artist based in Houston, helped me coordinate the ensemble. Terry had never before worked with the five musicians we secured. They did, however, work very well together.

Did they spend a significant amount of time rehearsing?

Terry traveled to Houston on a Monday and worked with them during the week leading up to the opening. It was important to me that Terry delivered the invocation to the exhibition on that Friday evening. His performance literally opened the show. With so many moving parts, there were many opportunities for things to go awry, and I needed a symbolic way to ritualize the opening—a calling of the ancestors, as it were, to bless the event and the events to follow.

It seems that Terry's performances were alive with ideas and energy. What was it like to be in the room for one? How did the audience respond? I assume that it was pretty magnificent to see his 18-foot long *Akrhaphones* in action.

It was a ritual. It was the calling of the ancestors. It set the tone for the exhibition. That piece, *The Last Trumpet*, was so powerful even beyond the wonder of those huge trumpets creating and emitting sound. Terry was working with the musicians to get an unexpected range of sounds out of the horns. And, of course, it was a pure spectacle because it was the Sacred Order of the Twilight Brothers. They came in with the monkey fur shawls, fezzes, and sashes. It felt like a Masonic group had come together and we were witnessing something very sacred. The space was packed with people and the group walked in with the trumpets and began playing them; it was amazing. And then Terry launched into a monologue about Bessie Smith and how she died, how she was denied treatment. It brought you into how this great woman and other great people, known and unknown, were considered "niggers." It was the sharp pointed edge of history—how the word "nigger" was used to wound and denigrate and then how that word became the root of other words. It was astounding for the public to hear someone say that word in this context. And not only say the word, but every hostile iteration of the word—evoking the histories of those words. It brought to the fore the shame of that history, as well as empowerment because our ancestors survived in spite of it all. It was about owning those histories and bringing them to the fore. It felt very assaultive, but in a way that was moving toward catharsis. When people walked out, they felt enlightened in strange ways. It was a very powerful performance.

It's a big regret not to have seen one of his performances in person. In this exhibition, I included documentation of *At Osiris* and *Postlude (Corpus Specere)*, the performances he did at The Studio Museum during *Radical Presence*, which were also some of his last. *Postlude (Corpus Specere)* conveyed a similar sense of the ritualistic purification you're talking about. Terry and the other performers walked in together, formed a circle by linking arms, and generated sound with their bodies via loud breathing and pounding on their own chests before they launched into playing their instruments and speaking. All the while, *Corpus Specere*, his video featuring horrific black-and-white photographs of lynched bodies, was projected in the background.

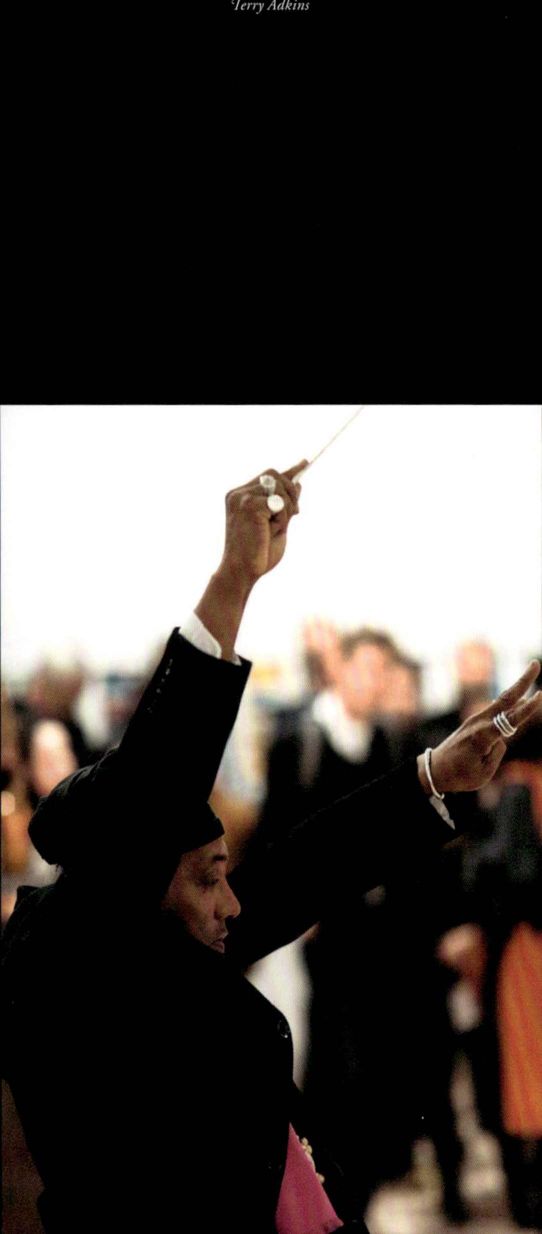

Terry Adkins

Have you seen that video, or many of Terry's other videos? If so, do any of them particularly resonate with you?

To be honest, no, I have not seen a lot of the videos.

After Terry's sudden passing, there was such an outpouring of love for him through memorials, articles, and online tributes. In *The Brooklyn Rail*'s article, "A Memory Jug for Terry Adkins," you cited Terry's belief in art's ability to change the world and said that "he did so." He undoubtedly had a profound influence on many people. Can you talk a bit about your view on his impact?

Terry was committed to reviving histories and finding new ways to share those histories. Because of that, people's legacies are alive and well today. For instance, his project on Lightnin' Hopkins at Project Row Houses was groundbreaking…and what it yielded was astounding! Terry not only celebrated this musical legend's work but also created a visual component to it that ran parallel to the artist's iconic musical form. Terry was able to transform the blues cadence into a visual language and present that to the world. The groundswell of Terry's work, and his digging into the archives, was amazing! He actually found people who knew Lightnin' Hopkins and found stories, crafted works, and created installations that really celebrated him and made people stop to think about the indelible impact this man had, not only on the city of Houston, but on the world. And because of that, the Texas Historical Commission actually erected a historical marker to Lightnin' Hopkins in Houston's Third Ward. That was directly due to Terry's efforts and his work. That's just one bit of evidence about how Terry, through his art and activism, made tangible changes to celebrate historical people who were icons.

Do you have a favorite memory with Terry?

Another crazy story was from when Terry and I both served on a panel for the United States Artists Fellowship Awards out in Los Angeles, California. I came in the night that Michael Jackson passed away, and I could barely get into downtown LA because of the convergence of people. I got in very late and just wanted to get into the bed and sleep. Just as I fell asleep, I heard footsteps overhead, pacing back and forth. I called the front desk to complain and I could tell that they sent someone up because it stopped. There was a lull, but it started up again. The next morning, I found out that it was Terry. He said he was working on something and that he needed to walk and talk to himself to figure things out. He literally paced all night. That next evening, Terry went out to walk. He was out all night. I don't know many people whose process is like that.

Even though he is physically gone from this earth, I hear Terry in my head from time to time. It's kind of crazy, but I know that I'm not alone. Who knows how long any of us have on this earth, but I think Terry understood that his time was limited. He crammed it all in! When people are relentless in their creative process, they tend to be very cognizant that they may have a finite amount of time. There was so much to be done and so little time to do it and he had to take every moment given. There was nothing frivolous about him.

Now, the man loved to shop though! He loved shoes and he loved his outfits. I can tell you that. They were part of the whole persona. More than anything else, he understood the power of the image and understood what he felt was his responsibility to keep memories and histories alive. I know he understood his capacity to change the world. He knew that instinctively. Maybe it comes from that long line of preachers and soul savers. He literally felt it was his responsibility to do something with the gifts that he had been given.

———

Valerie Cassel Oliver is Senior Curator at Contemporary Arts Museum Houston. She organized two exhibitions that featured Terry Adkins' work—Double Consciousness: Black Conceptual Art Since 1970 *and* Radical Presence: Black Performance in Contemporary Art, *which traveled extensively from 2013–2015.*

IAN BERRY

In Conversation with Kendra Paitz

KP: How did you and Terry first meet? Or when did you become aware of his work?

IB: I was aware of his work through images when I was in grad school; I had seen very few in person. We met in Williamstown, Massachusetts. My first curatorial post was at the Williams College Museum of Art, where we organized a symposium about race and education in 2000. Nayland Blake, James Luna, Tim Rollins, Carrie Mae Weems, and Deborah Willis, were all part of the event and they made a huge impact on me. I went on to be involved with all of them in different projects including organizing surveys of Nayland Blake and Tim Rollins + K.O.S. It was an inspirational and formative event for me.

When it was time for Carrie Mae to give her lecture, the lights went down and someone started playing a saxophone at the back of the room. It was Terry. It was a big surprise. He improvised and led her to the front of the room. She went to the podium and gave her presentation. Terry stayed for the rest of the weekend. I was entranced, as most people were when they met Terry. He was a seductive guy.

We hung out some that weekend and he immediately pitched me his work. I was a young curator hungry for that attention from an artist and we made a lasting connection. Over the years I saw him in Philadelphia and Brooklyn and he would keep me updated on shows, jobs, and kids. I remember when he got the job at Penn.

Our talks often revolved around Terry challenging me, asking why I was showing the artists I was showing, and telling me who I should be looking at. His challenges were revealing about his own evolving position about what it meant to be an artist in the world. Even if we would only talk once or twice a year, we would restart the conversation where we left off about politics, the art market, his work and who was and wasn't seeing it, other black artists and who was getting shows and why, students, teaching, and the university system. It started with an introduction from Carrie Mae Weems and I'm thankful for that.

That symposium happened because of Linda Shearer, then director at the Williams College Museum. She knew these artists from her experience running Artists Space and as a curator at museums in New York. In many ways, I was learning from Linda. She was generous to give me an assistant role in that event. It turned out to be critical to my understanding of art's power and possible roles in society.

What a rich history. I didn't realize that the two of you had known each other for so long. It's been such a gift to have these conversations because, although I met Terry and can connect some of the dots, the majority of my experience with him is secondhand.

One of the interesting things about Terry—which, I think maybe we've talked about before—is that, like

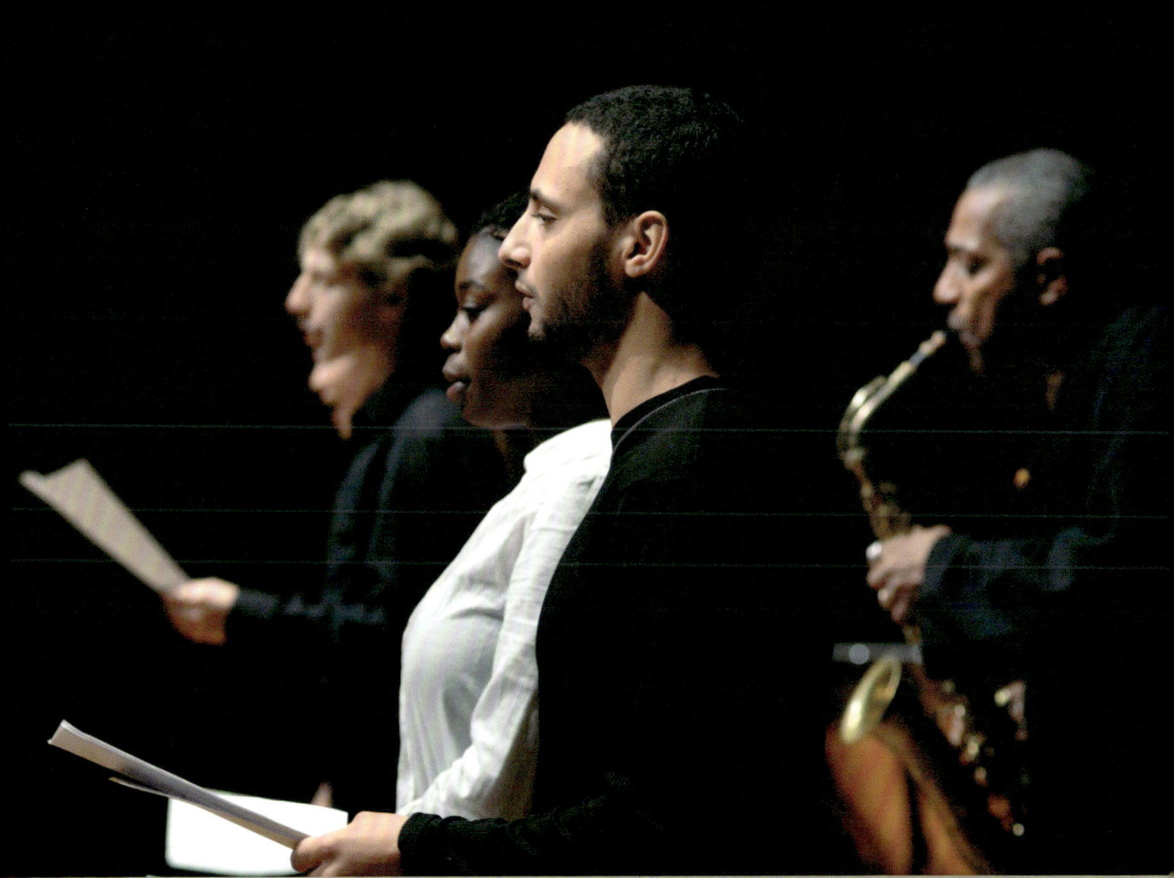

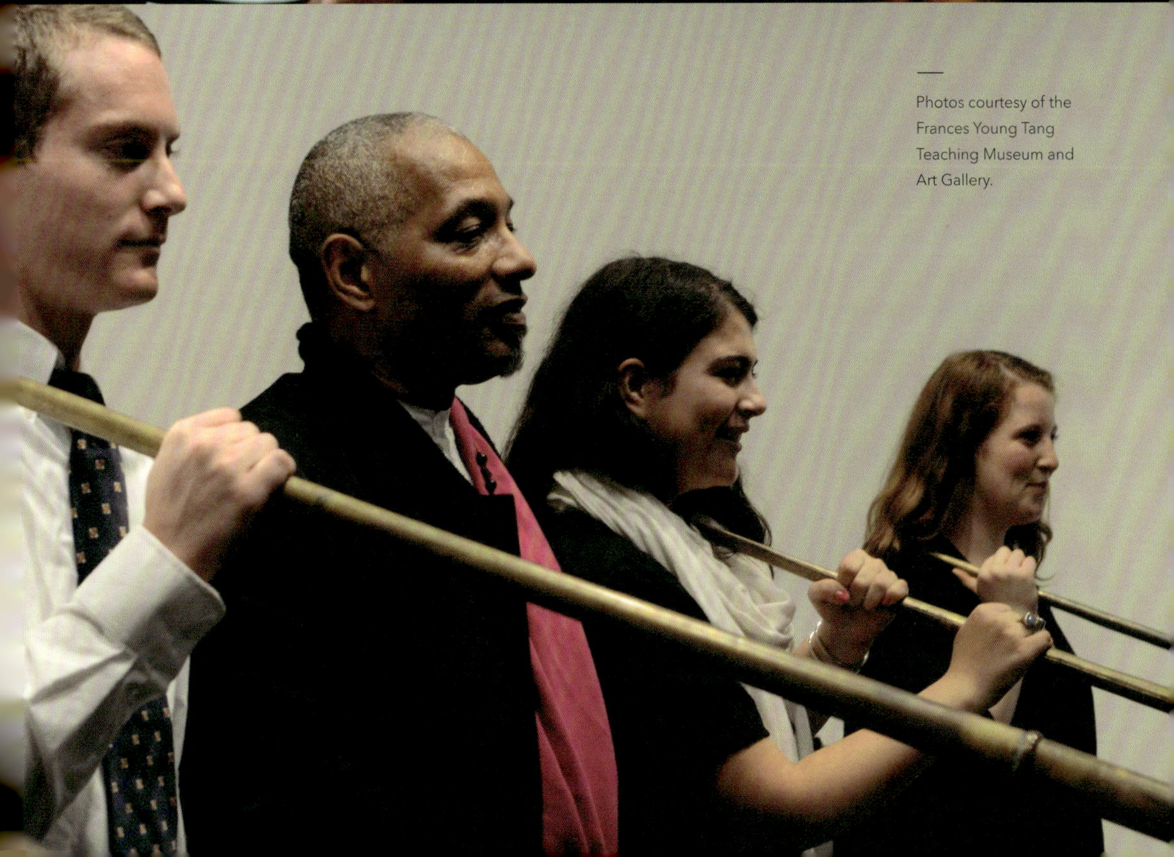

Photos courtesy of the
Frances Young Tang
Teaching Museum and
Art Gallery.

Carrie Mae and Nayland and a few other artists of his generation, he thought of his daily activities, decisions, and actions as part of his art practice. So, whether he took a teaching job at a certain place, or showed alongside a certain artist, or made other life choices, those choices were integral in every way to his conception of what it meant to be an artist in the world.

Those conversations in which he challenged me about what artists I was showing at the museum, or taking the art world to task about what was going on at art fairs and in magazines—I feel like that was part of his art. His art was meant to change the world, to change how we thought about history, individuals, race, and power. It happened not just through making and displaying sculptures, or giving lectures and teaching, but also in more private ways. In ways that maybe didn't look like artwork but that had huge impacts. I definitely thought and acted on things that didn't have to do with Terry's work because of his provocations.

Everyone that I've talked to has cited his influence on their thinking and/or making. They've talked about how he pushed them to be better, or to be more critical.

In a certain way, he came from a Duchampian trickster spirit space. Sometimes the provocation was to remind us to get out of our own expectations. He wasn't a careful activist at every turn. Sometimes yes, but other times he was jarring us so we would notice our own decision-making, or our looking, and our taste. It wasn't that he wanted us to decide one way or the other, necessarily, he wanted people to be more thoughtful.

You curated Terry's 30-year retrospective in 2012, which was long overdue. What prompted you to act at that moment, and how did you work together to plan the show?

As you said, it was long overdue. Because of my conversations with Terry, I knew that he had amazing work in storage. He didn't have regular gallery representation or consistent collectors. So, as a curator,

I saw an archive in danger of slipping away. They were artworks that needed to be seen and needed to be alive with interaction. Terry also regularly cannibalized his work. He would take parts from older pieces to make new ones; that was part of his process. I wanted to capture the memory of some of the works he was taking apart. That was the archival mission of the show but there were other missions. At that time, he was diving in, much more strongly, to alter egos and personas. He was playing with the performance of characters more than ever. It was an interesting shift that was somewhat invisible to the larger art world. I thought it was a strong part of his work that most people didn't know about. Our exhibition, *Recital*, was a way to think about recording some of that and to see how that work fit with the formal sculptures from his earlier years. I love those earlier forms and a lot of it is destroyed, but I wanted to see as much as I could. For me, and for the Tang Museum, our mission includes looking for these archives and pieces of art history that have been overlooked.

At the same time, race was becoming more and more a pressing issue for our students and faculty. Terry's work challenges the telling of race and history, particularly with the recitals on figures like John Brown, Bessie Smith, Lightnin' Hopkins, Matthew Henson, and the others we focused on in our show. That was important for students and faculty here to experience.

It was also an opportunity to give Terry support to complete new works. He finished a few big pieces that were bought by museums a couple of years later. We gave him fabrication help, got pieces out of storage, cleaned them up, photographed them, and recorded them. That's not always the most visible part of a museum show but it's important service to the artist.

You mentioned that race was becoming more of an issue on your campus. How did the students and faculty respond to Terry's work?

Everyone who participated was very moved. We presented two great performance pieces at Skidmore and he worked with students for both of them. Those students had life-transforming experiences. One of the performances was expansive, with guests like Kamau Patton and Clifford Owens, and huge projections on our music center stage. The other was a ceremonial playing of his long horns in the gallery by the students. The interactions in those moments were fantastic. The classes that interacted with the show and the museum audience that came in maybe considered John Brown's oratory for the first time, or Beethoven's race, or Jimi Hendrix's military record, or Matthew Henson's legacy as a polar explorer.

I'm always a little bit unsatisfied. That's something that Terry and I had in common. He was always unsatisfied. There's a level of abstraction in Terry's work that can sometimes make the research hard to access for newer or less close-looking museum audiences. I underestimated how hard it was for some people to access that content. That's something I learned. That kind of abstraction, that work that Terry wanted you to do as a viewer, which I think is so important, does push away some. The show had less of a campus effect than I hoped but I think it had individual and small group effects that were amazing and worth every minute.

I think you're right, the abstraction can make the work more difficult for broader audiences. Although you told me that Terry liked the magic and didn't like to reveal too much information, I had to write wall labels to provide that point of access for the extraordinary content. I found that our visitors were particularly fascinated by the slow transitions in *Synapse (from Black Beethoven)* and the flickering stereo cards set to Dr. King's speech and Jimi Hendrix's music in *Flumen Orationis*. You exhibited *Synapse* and a few other videos on smaller monitors. Were the reactions similar at the Tang or did people tend to gravitate more toward the sculptural works?

The smaller videos were a little tricky because the sound was on headphones. The stereo animation works because of that amazing mash-up of Martin Luther King Jr. and "Machine Gun." The cadences of those two things naturally flow together without much manipulation from Terry. He layered them on top of each other and realized how well they went together. If you didn't put the headphones on though, those were less accessed than they could have been in their own rooms, for instance.

The most provocative work in our show was the Beethoven music box sculpture that made a racket that really jarred you and got you out of your comfort zone. The way the room was arranged, you saw it and then turned a corner to reveal a sky-high stack of chair legs, which was a new sculpture at the time. That piece commanded your attention. And then you turned around to go to the next room or to leave and you'd see *Black Beethoven* again. Most people, at that point, would realize that there was something strange going on, which made the curiosity ramp up. *Black Beethoven* was very popular. And asks, "Was Beethoven black? What does that mean? How does that alter your understanding of him or his music?" If they hadn't accessed that kind of questioning of history yet in the show, that piece got them into that frame of thinking.

You're working on Terry's first large monograph. How involved was he in the planning process? Do you hear his voice in your head as you're making decisions?

Absolutely! Maybe I need to stop listening to that voice and get my work done. In many ways, Terry never finished anything. He didn't like objects, artworks, sculptures, or performances to have a conclusion. To him, they didn't have an end; they had a life. That's why it made sense to him to reorganize a piece or have interchangeable members of the Lone Wolf Recital Corps. Putting an end to something was against his mission. It was his love of improvisation, his love of challenge, his love of ever pushing forward, that things were never fixed. When something is fixed, he understood that power could enter into it. When something is fixed, somebody could own it, own that power. Terry was always challenging ownership and power.

It was hard to live in the world that way because everything else in our culture says that doesn't equal success. He had to give up a certain amount of market success and attention. That was a hard choice for him from time to time.

One of the reasons it was hard to get the book together was because we had a lot of conversations about what a book could be and we weren't done. How would a book record or display his unfixed-ness, when the whole reality of a book is a fixed thing? It's an object that gets published. There's a moment when it's set. He really wanted a book. I love books and wanted to do that for him, so there was no question about doing it or not doing it. It was about how to make a book that would best represent Terry's thinking. We looked at a lot of other artists' books and had great conversations about things that he liked and didn't like. I have a great sense of his design choices. The designer, Barbara Glauber, was able to meet Terry and see all of that too. I'm definitely hearing his voice.

Did he help select the writers?

Terry was intimately involved in selecting the writers. We had many conversations about who would write, who we should ask, whether to assign them topics or not, how much we should edit once they were done. It worked out well but he died right at the last stage of the writing. He saw all of the texts and personally edited most of them. He had direct interactions with all of the writers. I am very confident and excited about the writing in the book. I feel like Terry, in many ways, put his stamp on it. When I'm making the book, my goal is to listen to him, and that's why it took a long time to restart my energy for making it after he died. His voice is very strong and his death was a real shock. I was not at all prepared for that. There's a ton of stuff I didn't ask him that I was going to ask him. We're pushing through, but because of his interest in being unfixed, there are a lot of issues with titles and dates, and we had to figure out a system. We have photographs that we don't know exactly where they were taken or who the

photographer was. We're doing our best to put it together and make it in a way that Terry would appreciate.

I don't envy you that task at all. It's been so difficult to pull together the information just for these twelve videos. And so many dates and titles that have been published seem to be wrong. I've been sorting through listings in catalogues, permanent collections, and interviews, and having conversations with his colleagues and Merele. And thankfully Joshua Mosley still has some of their email correspondence and original source files; he actually made a new HD master copy of Synapse (from Black Beethoven) for our exhibition and the estate.

That's great.

Do you have a favorite memory with Terry?

One? I don't have one favorite; there are so many. That first memory of him as a mysterious figure in the back of the room was a perfect way to meet him. It was exactly his vibe. He was an unknowable ghost of history. I had many moments with him that were rough, when he would call me out about something. I learned it was one of his modes of communication, but it always rattled me. I would think, "Terry's upset about this. I've got to fix it." But we would talk things through and make it work. He wasn't a dictator. It was a two-way conversation and he was into the back and forth.

It's hard to talk about this without getting emotional. There were a few times when we would be somewhere and he would want to go outside to smoke. Those were moments when he could remove himself from an event and clear his head. I liked our conversations during those moments. Those were times when he wasn't so worried about performing. I think he was always on stage when other people were around, especially if it was a talk or symposium or dinner. I relished those moments when he relaxed a little bit and we talked about our families, our kids.

In his *Artforum* conversation with George Lewis, Terry said that what he "hoped distinguishe[d] [his] work from that of other artists by virtue of [him] being a musician" was the "idea of trace." Could you speak a little about the idea of trace in his work, or perhaps the traces he left behind?

Terry was very interested in living legacies. He was moved by human achievement. He was a researcher. Finding that Matthew Henson story, for example. He was impressed by a person who could accomplish all these things—as an inventor, explorer, engineer, etc. When Terry found these stories, they became living parts of his life and he wanted them to become living parts of our lives. He didn't simply promote or lecture about these people, he wanted to make them alive for us.

His experience of discovering a history, a story, a recording, a place (like when he went to Italy or the Arctic) was fuel. It was life-giving. He was resuscitating parts of history and challenging us to keep parts of it alive. How can you make John Brown's story alive today? How can you make the history of a street corner in Houston, Texas, animated or changed for the people living there? How do you best celebrate John Coltrane, Jimi Hendrix, or Beethoven? He left markers of those research moments. It's our job—the people who share Terry's goals—to figure out how to maintain those markers, pass on those stories, so more people are reminded of those traces.

———

Ian Berry is the Dayton Director at the Frances Young Tang Teaching Museum at Skidmore College in Saratoga Springs, New York. In 2012, he curated Recital, *Terry Adkins' 30-year traveling retrospective. He is currently overseeing production of Adkins' first large monograph.*

BIOGRAPHY

Terry Adkins (1953–2014)

Terry Adkins was born in Washington, D.C., and grew up in Alexandria, Virginia, with his parents and four siblings. He attended Fisk University (Nashville, Tennessee), where he studied with Martin Puryear and Aaron Douglas before graduating with a B.S. in Printmaking in 1975. He then received an M.S. in Printmaking from Illinois State University (Normal) in 1977, and an M.F.A. in Sculpture from University of Kentucky (Lexington) in 1979.

Adkins researched groundbreaking historical figures—such as John Brown, Matthew Henson, or Bessie Smith—whose legacies were in danger of being forgotten. A jazz musician who played the saxophone, he created a vast body of work that included sculptures, photographs, videos, prints, installations, and performances. Adkins said, "I try to make sculpture that is as ephemeral and transient as music is…And when it comes to working with sound…I try to make it more of a physical thing, so that embedded in the sculpture is the trace of sound, the trace of the nature of sound."[1] In 1986, Adkins founded the Lone Wolf Recital Corps, a collaborative group with rotating membership, with whom he performed dynamic combinations of spoken word, music, and song, within installations that often included costumes, sculpture, video, and (sometimes invented) instruments such as his 18-foot long *Akrhaphone* horns.

Adkins' work was recently presented in the 2015 *Venice Biennale*, the 2014 *Whitney Biennial*, and the traveling exhibition *Radical Presence: Black Performance in Contemporary Art*. In 2012, his thirty-year retrospective was organized by the Frances Young Tang Teaching Museum and Art Gallery at Skidmore College, Saratoga Springs, New York, and later traveled to the Mary & Leigh Block Museum of Art at Northwestern University, Evanston, Illinois. Adkins' work has also been exhibited at Palais de Tokyo, Paris; Museum of Contemporary Art, Chicago; American Academy in Rome; Eastern State Penitentiary, Philadelphia; Institute of Contemporary Art, Philadelphia; The Studio Museum in Harlem, New York; The Renaissance Society at the University of Chicago; and Contemporary Arts Museum Houston, among many others.

Adkins' work is in the collections of Tate Modern, London; The Studio Museum in Harlem, New York; Museum of Modern Art, New York; Metropolitan Museum of Art, New York; High Museum of Art, Atlanta; Hirshhorn Museum and Sculpture Garden, Washington, D.C.; and Jack S. Blanton Museum of Art, University of Texas at Austin. He was awarded the Jesse Howard, Jr. / Jacob H. Lazarus Metropolitan Museum of Art Rome Prize in 2009. Adkins was also awarded fellowships by the National Endowment for the Arts, Joan Mitchell Foundation, and New York Foundation for the Arts, among others.

A dedicated educator, Adkins taught briefly at University of Kentucky and California State University, Chico, before joining the faculty at State University of New York at New Paltz for eight years. From 2000–2014, Adkins was a professor in the Department of Fine Arts in the School of Design at University of Pennsylvania. He mentored a number of artists, including Demetrius Oliver, Jamal Cyrus, and Jacolby Satterwhite.

Adkins lived in Brooklyn, New York, with his wife, Merele Williams, and their children, Titus and Turiya. His estate is represented by Salon 94, New York.

---

1. Adkins, Terry. "Event Scores: Terry Adkins and George Lewis in Conversation." *Artforum International*, March 2014, 252.

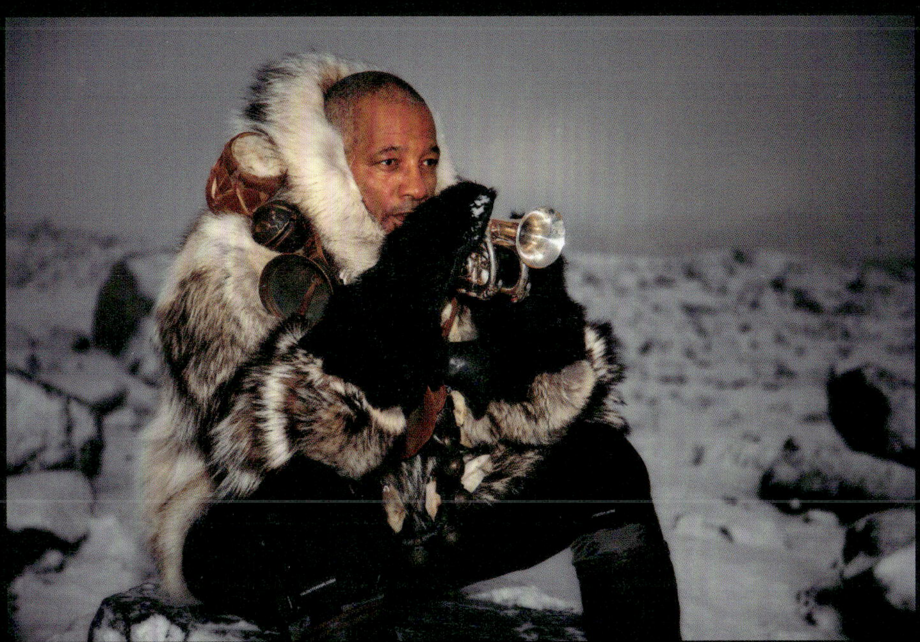

Portrait of Terry Adkins.
Copyright Chris Blade, 2013.
www.chrisblade.com

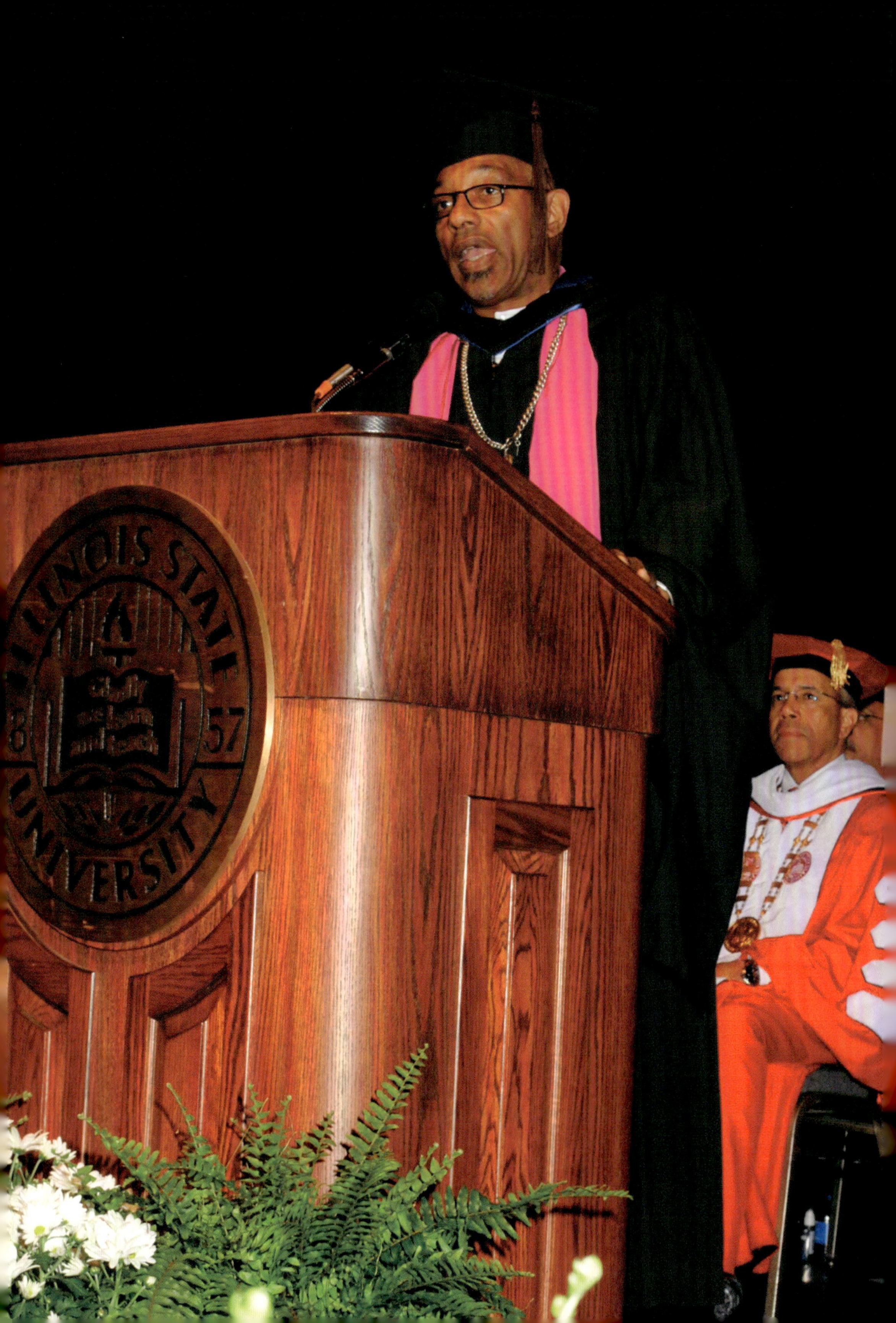

COMMENCEMENT ADDRESS

College of Fine Arts, Illinois State University, May 11, 2013

Adkins, who received his M.S. in Printmaking (1977) from Illinois State University's School of Art, delivered the 2013 College of Fine Arts commencement address and was also inducted into the College's Hall of Fame.

—

President Bowman, Dean Major, distinguished guests, alumni, faculty, family, friends, and graduating students. I am deeply touched by the distinguished capacity of being honored as the 154th commencement alumni guest speaker for the College of Fine Arts class of 2013. It is for me a great cardinal homecoming, teeming as it is with sentiments of the highest regard and with the perennial flourish of ceremony, grandeur, and celebration that mark the transitional magnitude of this most auspicious occasion. I first arrived at campus in the winter of 1975, having driven a rental van from my alma mater, Fisk University in Nashville, northward through ice, snow, and frigid temperatures so severe that I quickly discovered what the survival tactics of thermal underwear and layering were all about. I return today forever grateful for the excellent educational experiences that I received at this Midwestern oasis that is Illinois State University. She sharpened my mind, honed my gifts, opened my eyes, and tuned my heart to the humbling measure of responsibility that accompanies the great privilege of joining the ranks of an international consortium of young emerging professionals in the arts. Tonight I stand before you straddling fond memories of the past with a projected vision of hope for the future as you, our alumni to be, are now about to embark upon one of the most fascinating journeys of your life. Congratulations to the College of Fine Arts' class of 2013.

Congratulations are in order too for the other members of this eager-eyed assembly of heightened anticipation. Here's to the duly proud loved ones—parents, siblings, extended family, friends, and faculty gathered tonight in your honor. Their sacrifice of unwavering support for your creative endeavors springs from deep-seated faith and the promising certainty that you will indeed realize the fullest potential of your respective vocations in the years to come. What an ardent and reaffirming faith it is too, practiced most lovingly by your parents, whose devout and steadfast belief in the enduring value of an education in the arts transcends the practical concerns of their better judgment. They have stood by you in united gallantry, ignoring the harsh realities of the slim possibility that you might somehow make a decent living from your chosen calling. And yet, we must boldly face and firmly address the menacing questions that hover in the shadows of this joyful event. How will you survive with a higher education in the arts? How can your learning be meaningful or fulfilling in a turbulent world beset by catastrophe in every conceivable sphere of human experience? When I posed these questions in 1977 after being flung into the real world as you are about to be, the options were few, the circumstances dire. We had to resign ourselves to but two options—to either pursue an extended career in higher education through teaching or to make risky pilgrimage to thriving art centers to put our talents and ideals to the test against all odds in search of fame and fortune. Needless to say, extremely few of us emerged from the narrow end of the funneling tide with our career-laden dreams still intact.

Today the issues surrounding these questions and their rejoined consequences have become even more pervasive, complex, and exaggerated. The stakes have been raised; survival for young professional artists, composers, musicians, playwrights, and actors seems to be an even more insurmountable undertaking than it was 36 years ago when I was in your shoes. The sign of the times in reign of quantity that presently engulfs us has shaped an age characterized by the stutter and mounting brevity of time collapsed into space, wherein quantity overwhelms quality; information is more valued than knowledge; image veils a lack of substance; success is equated with wealth; mediocrity is propped up as genius; the billionaire is the hero of modern life; even the intrinsic value of the arts is constantly threatened by the encroachment of monetary rank, merited by the degree to which they are usurped and regurgitated by the gigantic. But fear not. Fortunately, the alarming rise of these monstrous deviations has coincided with the advancement of promising alternatives that hopefully signal the dawning of our recovery from them.

The expanded fields of the arts have openly embraced an interdisciplinary ideal, dissolving longstanding boundaries and incorporating the underlying principles and strategies from other bodies of knowledge as never before. Under the banner of creative research, one commonly finds imaginative arts practitioners employing methodologies normally ascribed to immersive studies in science, history, architecture, politics, design, archeology, literature, activism, and sociology, among others. These tendencies coupled with redefining developments in platforms for global communication have revolutionized the flow of information, transformed the matrix for the exchange of creative ideas, and given access to burgeoning audiences for the arts. Mind you, these virtual conveniences are only tools, prospects for asserting your voice in the world. There is

no substitute for the discipline, rigor, and devotion to craft that must fuel your quest for aspiring to attain the standards of excellence embodied in the timeless masterworks of our artistic heritage.

Nor does the facile access to massive amounts of information come without a charge of vital responsibility. The limitless palette of life can never be truly grasped through the envelope of a computer screen. Data is merely compiled material that must be filtered through the sieve of unquantifiable human experience in order to be transformed into discerning critical knowledge. Accordingly equipped, you can help to pry the arts away from their being reduced to dangling modifiers of societal excess to once again becoming urgent spiritual necessities for all, driven by the purpose of reflecting upon the myriad dimensions of what it means to be human today. Walt Whitman (1819–1892) beautifully encapsulates the transcendent universals that comprise what he calls this "vast similitude" in his poem "On the Beach at Night Alone":

—

On the beach at night alone,

As the old mother sways her to and fro singing her husky song,

As I watch the bright stars shining, I think a thought of the clef of the universes and of the future.

A vast similitude interlocks all,

All spheres, grown, ungrown, small, large, suns, moons, planets,

All distances of place however wide,

All distances of time, all inanimate forms,

All souls, all living bodies though they be ever so different, or in different worlds,

All gaseous, watery, vegetable, mineral processes, the fishes, the brutes,

All nations, colors, barbarisms, civilizations, languages,

All identities that have existed or may exist on this globe, or any globe,

All lives and deaths, all of the past, present, future,

This vast similitude spans them, and always has spann'd,

And shall forever span them and compactly hold and enclose them.

—

Our questions yet remain. How will you survive with an education in the arts? In most any way that you choose. How can a career in the arts be meaningful and fulfilling in a turbulent world? However you see fit to make it so. We need to hear from the talented and struggling voices of your generation. We want to see what happens when your creative imaginations clash with the realities of our existence. We want to know what you critically think and how you passionately feel about contemporary life on this small planet. The degrees that will soon be conferred upon you are not only important milestones in your gifted young lives. They are also an urgent call to arms.

Go forth from this place emboldened by your accomplishments to state your dream and stake your claim to the promising future that awaits you. Imagine it. Harness it. Realize it with integrity. Its authorship is in your hands; the choices are all up to you. Keep the faith. Thank you.

Terry Adkins Memorial Scholarship for Diversity

The School of Art at Illinois State University has created an endowed scholarship to honor the memory of alumnus Terry Adkins, who received his M.S. degree in Printmaking in 1977. The Terry Adkins Memorial Scholarship for Diversity will help art majors from traditionally underrepresented populations pursue their education in the School of Art.

The School of Art provides a professional and academic education for students desiring careers in the visual arts. Fully accredited by the National Association of Schools of Art and Design, the School of Art offers the following degrees: B.F.A., B.A., and B.S. in Studio Arts, Graphic Design, Art History, and Art Teacher Education; M.A. in Visual Culture; M.S. in Art Education; and M.F.A. in Studio Arts.

To make a donation, please visit advancement. illinoisstate.edu/terryadkins to pay by credit card. You can also send a check made out to Illinois State University, with "Terry Adkins Memorial Scholarship" in the memo line. Mail to:

———

Terry Adkins Memorial Scholarship for Diversity
c/o School of Art
Campus Box 5620
Illinois State University
Normal, IL 61790-5620

ACKNOWLEDGMENTS

by Kendra Paitz

Several of us had the opportunity to meet Terry Adkins, a distinguished alumnus of our School of Art, when he was here in 2013 to offer the College of Fine Arts' commencement address. With his profound intelligence and vibrant personality, he made a distinct impact during his short time on campus. Over the course of his career, Adkins created an incredibly complex and fearless body of work that illuminated the legacies of historical figures. It has been an honor to organize this exhibition and publication to tell a portion of his rich story.

I am grateful to Merele Williams for her gracious support of this project, from her immediate embrace of the idea, to her helpful assistance with research materials, to her engaging visit to the exhibition.

In a true testament to Adkins' impact on those around him, his friends and colleagues have been thoughtful, open, and generous participants in the conversations printed in this book. It has been a pleasure to learn more about this "unknowable ghost of history" (as Ian Berry referred to him) from some of those who knew him well. I am grateful to Lorna Simpson, Ian Berry, Joshua Mosley, Demetrius Oliver, and Valerie Cassel Oliver, for sharing their honest stories, astute analyses, and favorite memories. Ian and Joshua have also provided invaluable information since the earliest stages of this project. Thanks are also due to Joshua for his technical assistance, including the rendering of a new HD master copy of one of the videos.

I would like to thank Alissa Friedman at Salon 94, New York (which represents the artist's estate), who was instrumental to the initiation and realization of this exhibition. Thank you also to Jeanne Greenberg Rohatyn at Salon 94. I also appreciate the assistance that Jonathan Gardenhire and Mika Harding at Salon 94 provided with research materials and digital files. Gina Guddemi and Liz Gwinn at The Studio Museum in Harlem helpfully facilitated the loan of videos documenting Adkins' 2013 Lone Wolf Recital Corps performances at the Museum. Ian Berry, Jean Egger, and Sarah Miller at the Frances Young Tang Teaching Museum and Art Gallery kindly loaned documentation of Adkins' 2012 performance at their institution.

We, in the College of Fine Arts, are thrilled to have been able to initiate and endow the Terry Adkins Memorial Scholarship for Diversity (see page 105) in time for the exhibition's opening reception. Michael Wille, Director of the School of Art; Nancy Fewkes, Assistant to the Director of the School of Art; Barry Blinderman, Director of University Galleries; and Jean MK Miller, Dean of the College of Fine Arts, enthusiastically raised funds and promoted awareness about Adkins' life and work. At the time of this writing, the first scholarship has just been awarded to Alissa Palmer, a BFA student who is studying painting.

I appreciate our partners at Illinois State University's Milner Library—Kathleen Lonbom, Steve Koehler, Ross Griffiths, Li Rong, Magdalena Casper-Shipp, and Dean Dane Ward—for organizing a satellite screening of Adkins' *Synapse (from Black Beethoven)* that played continuously during the exhibition. Thank you to Ben

Libert and Janis Swanton in Research and Sponsored Programs and Laurie Merriman in the College of Fine Arts, who are always so helpful as we submit our external grants for consideration. Our collaboration with faculty and students in Art Education yielded lively educational materials and workshops. Thank you to Associate Professor Judith Briggs and students Kayla Hueneburg Aykuz, Keri Leach, and Anna Jahncke. Greg Swank and Micah Kuchan in Learning Spaces and AV Technologies helpfully loaned necessary equipment.

I cannot imagine a better partner for this book than Andrew Bybee. His intelligent and sensitive design, enthusiastic embrace of the project, and kind spirit have yielded a publication that elegantly celebrates Adkins' life and work. I am also indebted to my wonderful friend and colleague, Vanessa Meikle Schulman, for her diligent proofreading and continued support. She also pointed out the connection between Herman Melville and John Brown that I referenced in the description of *Behold Harpers Ferry*. I appreciate the professional service from Tiffany Chatham Smith and Linda Peltier-Moore at Regent Publishing. Thank you also to Jennifer Hsu at Lorna Simpson Studio for providing valuable assistance with catalogue materials.

I would like to express my sincere and unending gratitude to University Galleries' dynamic staff, without whom none of this would have been possible. We are a small staff and we work tirelessly to support each other's visions for projects, as well as our collective vision for the institution. Director Barry Blinderman, who offers insightful and attentive feedback about written materials, importantly secured a key donation for the memorial scholarship. Curator Jason Judd was integral to organizing and streamlining the technical components of the exhibition, was a good-humored partner for installation, and took great care in documenting the show. Registrar Gabe Johnson carefully processed all the paperwork, assisted with the installation, and painstakingly created the beautiful vinyl lettering that greeted exhibition visitors. Camron Johnson was very helpful with painting and lighting. Our interns, graduate students, and student workers also helped with the installation in countless ways: Reeti Mathur, Chrissy LaMaster Doty, Sierra Moore, Adam Epps, Rebecca Davis, Ernest Gardner, and Kayla Scott. Jason Hoffman also provided wonderfully skilled installation assistance.

I am especially grateful to The Andy Warhol Foundation for the Visual Arts for providing the critical funding for the exhibition and catalogue to honor Terry Adkins' powerful legacy. May his voice continue to resonate for generations to come.

CREDITS

This catalogue was published in conjunction with the exhibition *Terry Adkins: Soldier Shepherd Prophet Martyr: Videos from 1998–2013*, curated by Kendra Paitz, and presented at University Galleries of Illinois State University from February 23 through April 3, 2016.

This exhibition and publication have been made possible by a critical grant from The Andy Warhol Foundation for the Visual Arts. Programs at University Galleries are supported in part by a grant from the Illinois Arts Council Agency.

Publisher: University Galleries of Illinois State University, Normal, Illinois
Editor: Kendra Paitz
Designer: Andrew Joseph Bybee
Proofreaders: Vanessa Meikle Schulman and Barry Blinderman
Printer: Regent Publishing Services, Ltd., San Diego. Printed in China.
Distributor: Distributed Arts Publishers, New York, New York www.artbook.com
ISBN: 978-0-945558-37-8
Cover image: Terry Adkins, still from *Nutjuitok II* (detail), 2012. Single-channel digital video with sound.
Back cover image: Portrait of Terry Adkins. © Chris Blade, 2013. www.chrisblade.com
Photo credits: Illinois State University, page 102. Jason Judd, pages 58–69. Thank you to Jason for also creating the video stills used on pages 8–57 and 84. All other photo credits are listed in the image captions.

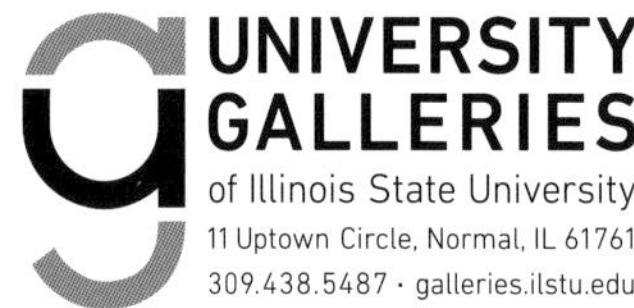

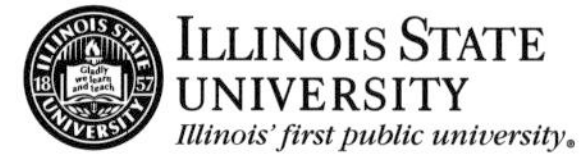

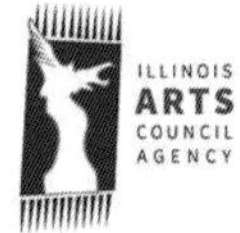